PELICAN BOOKS

God Is Not Yet Dead

Vítězslav Gardavsky was born in Ostrava, Czechoslovakia, in 1923 and graduated from the Charles University in Prague. As a Marxist atheist he was involved in the so-called Christian-Marxist Dialogue during the 1960s, which was often based in Czechoslovakia. *God Is Not Yet Dead* first appeared in German in 1968, following articles published in a Prague literary magazine, *Literárm noviny*, from 1966 to 1967. In 1968 Professor Gardavsky retired from his post as Professor of Philosophy at the Brno Military Academy.

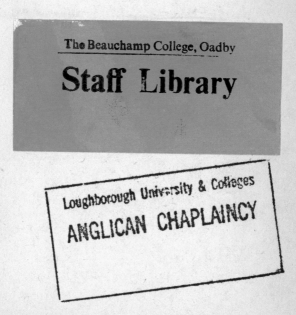

VÍTĚZSLAV GARDAVSKY

GOD IS
NOT YET DEAD

TRANSLATED FROM THE GERMAN
BY VIVIENNE MENKES

Centre for
Faith and Spirituality
Loughborough University

PENGUIN BOOKS

Penguin Books Ltd, Harmondsworth, Middlesex, England
Penguin Books Inc., 7110 Ambassador Road, Baltimore, Maryland 21207, U.S.A.
Penguin Books Australia Ltd, Ringwood, Victoria, Australia

First published 1973
This translation copyright © Vivienne Menkes, 1973

Made and printed in Great Britain
by Hazell Watson & Viney Ltd,
Aylesbury, Bucks
Set in Intertype Lectura

CONTENTS

INTRODUCTION

Digging Down to the Roots

Credo quia absurdum

Saying dating from the time of the Church Fathers

I do not believe, although it is absurd – a present-day Marxist might offer this twist on Tertullian's maxim as he meditates on his own period. But why? declared atheists will ask. Has it already become less absurd today to believe in God? Are we rushing headlong towards a time when we will forget everything and return to the faith of our fathers?

And by asking questions of this type they will suddenly grasp exactly what the maxim stirs up in them.

But not so fast! There may be more to it than just a witty paradox. It is possible that it really is easier today to believe in God and miracles than not to believe in them.

The maxim protests against the idea that believing or not believing is a simple matter. It expresses the point of view of the atheist who is familiar with the voices of the sirens enticing him into the deep waters of religion. It also expresses the spirit of adventure felt by a man who knows exactly what he is saying when he refuses to believe in God in spite of everything. The saying as we have formulated it is rooted in the Marxist atheist's spiritual equipment, which prevents him from surrendering to the threats of history or capitulating to the ordinary triviality of everyday existence. It is an attempt to remain true to oneself in this temporary world of ours, in these temporary times.

1

Man has hurled himself into the universe. We can think of flight round the earth as technically mastered; and now a landing on the moon. At the same time we are putting sounding-balloons into orbit to other planets in our solar system. All this gives rise to a wealth of technical optimism. The cosmic age has begun. We can look beyond the threshold of our own earthly home into boundless space. What will man be out there? What is our identity in the vast gulfs of the cosmos? We want to know, or we must lose all hope.

We have split the atom and can penetrate the secrets of the microstructure of matter. The energies we have discovered there and those we have yet to discover surpass all our ideas about the possibility of annihilation, but they also surpass our ideas about the possibility of enrichment. Here, too, technical optimism prevails, but it puts us into a predicament. If I – as a representative of mankind – am annihilated, what will this lead to? If I become exorbitantly rich, who will I be?

The same questions arise in the field of cybernetics, which is developing so promisingly. If automated machines, those creatures of the scientific and technological revolution, relieve me of the need to spend the greater part of my life in a state of alienation, what will I make of the offers and temptations of freedom? How far are they connected with mankind?

The door leading to the secrets of life has been opened just a crack, after remaining closed for so long. Whatever we know in this field – though so far it is more a question of surmising rather than actually knowing – leads us to a pinnacle of hope, but it also arouses a feeling of horror at the possibilities of abuse. Man develops from within. If we want to calculate how much we have developed, there is still an element of uncertainty. The cosmic age, the atomic age, the cybernetic age, the age of biology . . .

Those are the paths along which man has travelled in the twentieth century. Scientists are not entirely clear about how they are going to continue or where they will lead to. Contradictory alternatives; predictions bursting with confidence; the same predictions, but now full of despondency; decisions involving the gravest responsibility; hesitation in the face of risks; risks resulting from hesitation; portentous red push-buttons; uncertain experts; questions, yet more questions. And the most important remain unanswered. The days when scientists were full of naïve self-confidence are over, and they no longer think of the world as small enough to take in at a glance and relatively easy to control. As modern science and technology evolve, they offer an image which looks more and more like one huge question-mark.

As the questions become more urgent, the demand for answers grows more urgent as well. Is there any possibility that answers will be found? All we know is that greater efforts are being made to find them. Even the modernized version of Christianity makes no promises. But it does offer a sort of core of certainty. What have those who have no god got to offer?

2

Meanwhile our world lives in its own present. It appears to be posing a totally different set of questions. It is not on a cosmic scale. Men live out their life in greater depth and with greater immediacy. Politics. Happiness. Conflicts; constant international tensions; wars breaking out first at one end of the globe and then at the other.

The whirlwind which stirs up the conflicts overrunning our planet never lets up for a moment either. It turns faster, faster, sucking millions of people into its dangerous maelstrom. Conflicts the length of the meridian and in every degree of latitude, forming a sort of cross of disputes. This means that the situation has become extraordinarily complicated. The points of contention pile up. Some of them cannot be put off much longer. And yet mankind seems to be becoming progressively less capable of solving them. They drag on, for years and for decades, some of them giving the impression that any idea of a solution in the foreseeable future is hopeless.

And there are no more sheltered spots away from the wind, wherever we live.

The accumulated burden of information weighs on our consciousness day in and day out, although scarcely anything has happened anywhere. And so something which is in fact intended to increase our political awareness and stir us to action becomes only too often a factor which turns the event into an everyday occurrence and allows us to become totally indifferent to it. Every evening the horrors of war, tragedies, catastrophes are the permanent accompaniment of our daily lives.

As conflicts and incidents are repeated, we become correspondingly less capable of coping with them. We simply cannot live through them any longer in all their appalling topicality. We think that the 'time is out of joint' and try to set against the abnormality of the age some element of normality tailored to the simple scale of an ordinary, commonplace, happy life. We shut the doors; we search for ways of insulating ourselves from the hubbub of the world outside.

But sooner or later we will realize that sheltered spots like this are pure fiction. And yet people still try, over and over again, to find them, with a determination which is worthy of a better cause.

From their hiding-place behind a screen or on a couch they see the world as hostile, irritating, dangerous – and irrational. They long to escape. They draw a magic circle of possessions round them. They swear loud and long by gods both great and small. They have been uprooted and yet they want to go on living. Our age is not merely the age of science, it is also the age of mythologies.

In these circumstances there is no doubt that it is more difficult to be a Marxist and an atheist than it used to be. We refuse to consider the world solely from the angle that it is absurd. We support the theory that understanding leads to action, not to suffering. We reject fictitious remedies and make preparations for real remedies, with varying degrees of success. But this rejection does not get rid of the problem. The people we want to win over are the very people who will not be satisfied with any old answer. But this means that we must get down to the root reasons underlying our conception of a world without God, of mankind untrammelled by myths. But what exactly does getting down to the root reasons involve?

3

In recent history the word 'radical' has taken on an emotional overtone of extremism. It is generally accepted as a combination of two elements: on the one hand it refers to protest by an individual or a group accompanied by starry-eyed and unworldly demands, and on the other hand it describes the concept of 'being revolutionary'.

But in its original meaning – and this is how it was always used by Marx – 'radical' means 'digging down to the roots'. For Marx, being radical was one of the crucial aspects of revolutionary activity. It does not simply mean a thorough uprooting of outdated rules and regulations and clearing the ground for new seed to be sown. The radical revolution is also permanently preoccupied with its own roots, trying to find out how firmly they are anchored in the soil of history, how they manage to grow up through the top-soil, how they thrust their way down into historical strata which lie ever deeper, absorbing the nutrients which have accumulated there over the centuries. This means that the growth of the stem and corolla of a revolution, which confirms that it can bear precious and nutritious fruit, always depends on whether its hidden roots grow and branch out evenly in all directions. Any social fact which is not rooted in the soil of history – or only very tenuously so – is always in danger of being destroyed: as soon as it has absorbed the nourishment offered by the recent past, it starts to wither away, even though it may go on bearing green leaves for some time yet.

This image may well be the most telling way of describing the growth of any type of society, and will therefore be equally applicable to a socialist society. If we agree among ourselves that socialism is the firm soil in which contemporary history is rooted, representing a practical effort by millions of men and women whose aim is to supply answers to *questions*, answers, that is, which are both worthy of mankind and in the final analysis generally acceptable – we will lump them together and refer to them in general terms as 'communism' – then tending its future development must include concern about the extent to which socialism as a modern phenomenon is rooted in history, which after all embraces several thousands of years.

If we reflect on this problem from time to time, socialism as a phenomenon of the modern era appears to be identical with its political significance, or rather identifiable with it. At any rate, it cannot be disputed that socialism, the various socialist systems in the world, the international communist movement, are important milestones along the path of social progress in our own century, and that taken jointly they form its historical axis. But it is far from self-evident that for this reason alone socialism and communism constitute an equally significant entity from the *historical* point of view. Now it is perfectly natural that *we* should see it in this way, but there is no reason why the non-communist world should do so, and indeed they don't. Rather the reverse, for they have thought of communism for many decades now as a foreign body lodged in history, an experiment which happens to have worked, but which will either disappear in time or else be swept away, as so many other movements have been.

Even if we take into account the class interest and class hatred which limit their understanding of the historical meaning of socialism, there is still one striking fact to be considered: a feeling engendered by the fact that 120 years of socialism and its attendant conflicts have not been enough for it to take root in the soil of European history, and indeed in world history.

We communists can put forward a large number of arguments against this reasoning. But we must still take a good deal of the blame ourselves. It seems that what we have called the root elements – elsewhere they tend to be referred to as the revolutionary tradition – have lost much of their power in recent years. The basic elements of the historical process have been divided into two groups – progressive and reactionary – in a fairly arbitrary way. The 'reactionary' elements were rejected out of hand, although we were not really in a position to deal with them and analyse them subjectively, whereas we tried to hurry the 'progressive' elements along too severely, hoping to find in them various nutrients which in fact they never possessed.

So the radical aspect of socialism seems to be something more than just a short-circuit of revolutionary traditions. It is rather its faculty for converting into nutrients all the various components of the soil of history, and for thrusting down in a burst of growth into the bowels of history, and at the same time thrusting upwards to form stem, corolla and fruit. That too – and in fact in the dialectics of this type of historical process of growth, that *alone* – represents the creative aspect of history; anything new – i.e. scientific, technical or artistic phenomena, a change in the political balance of power, or some form of progress – is not considered sufficiently stable unless it is related to all the various elements which add up to the value of history to humanity.

The radical conversion of everything in the soil of history does not of course involve taking absolutely everything over indiscriminately; instead it must be *integrated* to comply with the very essence of socialism, with its inherent laws and its spiritual equipment. It is just this integration from the class point of view which can make a specific contribution to the creative aspect of the history of man; it can participate actively in it, in a way which justifies socialism in the eyes of ordinary men and women just as much as its past economic or political successes or its military might. The universal attraction of socialism is in direct proportion to its radical content.

4

If we now have a good look round to see what we are actually rooted in and how deeply, we will find a good deal of information in the labour movement itself. Without it a whole host of contemporary facts – civilizing facts connected with culture, society and politics – are scarcely conceivable.

But we will go further and say that even the political and intellectual rise of the bourgeoisie in its 'heroic age' of the struggle against the might of theocratic feudalism now seems close to us and intelligible. We share Engels's admiration for the Renaissance – though with reservations. The Reformation has a special significance for us Czechs and Slovaks, for our ancestors were among the first to herald its arrival.

But that is not all by a long chalk: here we have Europe, not as a geographical concept, but as a historical one; Europe and its complicated, often thoroughly ambivalent significance for the world as a whole; classical antiquity as well as the Renaissance, Judaism and Christianity as well as the Reformation. Until recently we simply thought of classical antiquity as antique – a few excavations, a few ruins, Schliemann, the ruins of Troy, the myths of Prometheus and Antaeus, Ovid's advice on love-making, Caesar and his division of Gaul into three parts, Seneca dying. . . . And a few relics of living

Latin speakers. Latin in Church and in the hospital and – along with ancient Greek – in the dictionary.

Europe and its influence on the world is difficult to understand unless we consider it in conjunction with the world of the ancient Greeks and Romans; similarly, socialism and Communism – if we think of them as a good deal more than a specific system of economics and power politics – cannot be established unless we consciously and repeatedly incorporate into them these nutrients which are so essential to us. It is true that they constitute only a part of the basic elements we need for our nourishment and cannot be given an exaggerated preference over the other elements, but they must still be taken into account.

The same applies to Judaism and Christianity, though here the situation is much more complicated. All that has survived of classical antiquity is a sort of spiritual realm and a few ruins for tourists to visit. Christianity, on the other hand, is a living organism abounding in ambition which intervenes as much in everyday events today as it did a thousand years ago. Is it going through some sort of crisis? Is it enjoying a boom? At any rate, there it is, with all its rich past. It is there, silent but ever-present in buildings, in treasuries bulging with gold, in museums and collections, in the silhouettes of houses and cities. It is there, melted down and hidden, in customs, ethical standards, in proverbs and metaphors, in songs. It is there – anonymously this time – as the basic material for certain structures, even if they have been melted down and recast.

But it is also there as a living and functioning presence. It is not merely a spiritual presence, one of the historical dimensions of the European; it is also a physical presence, an institution, Church, organization, political interest; it sometimes says 'No!' to facts to which millions of people devote all their energies, and at other times says 'Yes!' to actions which those same millions think of as alien and hostile.

It is present as a profound inner belief for hundreds of thousands of people in this country and millions of people throughout the world, who have chosen it to guide their lives and to provide the basic motivation underlying all their actions. It is also present in the atheist's denial. And as a political force.

And yet, although our relationship to Christianity may be primarily political for a long time to come – and it can scarcely be otherwise – this does not let us off the question of whether Christianity has a historical meaning for socialism, and, if so, what sort of meaning. But it does in the end seem patently obvious that until we are capable of making a fair assessment of the epoch-making phenomenon that is Christianity we shall not be able to establish how far it has failed to measure up to its own inner potential in individual situations, by holding aloof from the realm of politics and the world-wide class war – indeed it often continues to do so now – to an extent which cannot be reconciled with the efforts at progress being made by mankind in our time; by defending the whole of its past history simply because it is worried about its political prestige; by not being capable of digging down to its own roots.

But the question of what exactly the relationship is between socialism, Communism and Christianity does not stem merely from the need for a political and ideological feud tinged with class warfare. It stems from the inner needs of the Communist movement, which is after all there for all men and women, for an epoch, for the change-over from a makeshift set-up permanently threatened by imminent catastrophe to a reorganized society. The Marxist is convinced that Christianity as a religious movement can be altered to fit in with socialism, with the tasks it has set itself, and its aims. But he knows that for many people who live under socialism and are busy constructing a socialist system, or are still at the stage of fighting for one, belief in God still cannot be altered. He knows that socialism is merely a transitional stage. He also knows that God is not quite dead. So what is God? Where are the blind spots in socialism? Where is the silence lurking behind a question-mark in Marxism? Where, in terms of our convictions, are the chasms which are even more unfathomable than those of Christianity? What human incentives can act more effectively on behalf of mankind – by means of their truthfulness and range – than belief in God?

If we once make up our minds to ask this type of question, Christianity stops being something alien, remote and dead. We no longer feel the need to steer well clear of it. The fear which for some unknown reason has been dogging us vanishes. Our anti-theism loses its weakness. We will find out about everything which has made Christianity remain vigorous even today, and about every-thing which makes certain sectors of the world population find it necessary – and as we acknowledge our own shortcomings, we will also get a clear picture of all those aspects which are garbled by socialism and its spiritual world. From then on we will no longer be indifferent to Christianity, politically or historically. We will feel the urge to analyse it and soak it up along with every other living and life-giving element in the age-old history of man.

5

The decision to dig to the roots has some point if we inquire in a thoroughly concrete and matter-of-fact way into the values which have been created by Christianity, into the inspiration it offers. A condescending and arrogant denial, quite apart from being thoroughly uncritical, is unworthy of the intellectual status of Marxism.

So what can the Bible offer the Marxist? What does Jesus mean to us? What exactly is the Word of God that is ascribed to him? What is the attitude of Marxist thought to such important Christian thinkers as St Augustine, St Thomas Aquinas, or Pascal? What do we make of medieval Christianity?

These questions may seem rather peculiar to atheist readers: after all, they virtually belong to the realm of theology!

Of course; and that is why they are an essential part of any self-critical study of contemporary Christian theism. But the same arguments compel even the Marxist atheist to sit up and think. He too must examine himself critically if he wants to be something more than a simple-minded God-denier.

That is why I have divided this book into three sections. In 'Monuments' I reflect on Christianity's historical heritage and ask myself what significance it can have for us non-believers. The second section, which I have called 'Theism Takes a Look at Itself', aims to give Marxist readers (though it is not directed exclusively to them) some insight into the way Christianity (Roman Catholicism in particular) sees itself, its objective position in the world today, and its prospects. The third and final section takes a look at us, at what we call Marxist atheism, and at what seems to us to be the basis of all our views on man, the world and history. I have called it 'Atheism Takes a Look at Itself'.

I am well aware of the difficulties involved. Marxism has not so far worked out its attitude to a large number of problems. So this book can claim to do no more than consider the various questions and encourage further reflection along the same lines. Such reflection is needed. In this age which is both full of hope and full of despair, two theses hold good, fitting together like the obverse and reverse of the same coin:

> *God is not quite dead.*
> *Man is not quite alive.*

Part 1

MONUMENTS

JACOB

Choice and Personal Identity

1

Write about the Bible! I must admit that the idea rather alarms me. We are dealing here with a book some thousands of years old, which tells of mythical incidents and memorable events in the far distant past. We read it in the evenings and allow ourselves to fall under the spell of the simplicity and the naïve and happy confidence which accompanies the tales of passion, cunning, deceit, murder, bloodthirsty rage, devotion, self-sacrifice, daring, fighting, enmity and tenderness. We are captivated by its profound human wisdom, that is sometimes bitter, sometimes full of hope. We are fascinated by the abundance of life – though life is much too short and far too steeped in suffering – which pervades the poetry of the psalms and love-songs as much as the fervour of the prophets. But there is more to it than that; we are daunted by the idea of treating the Bible as if it were just a piece of writing, because we must always remember that this book is a silent compendium of everything which the different peoples of the world as they came and went have learnt from their own experience and from the battles they have fought, and then set down, whenever they sought advice, support, arguments against their enemies, an explanation for something that had happened, peace for their troubled minds, the hope that tomorrow will be better than today. The Bible has been read countless times during the hundreds of years since it was written, and from each period it has assimilated and preserved something of importance to mankind: new songs have been composed, incidents have been given a new lease of life, apocryphal revisions have been made, pieces of sculpture and valuable paintings have been produced. So the message which it brings to mankind has grown more fertile all the time. And so the legacy of the nations of the past is handed down to the new nations as they appear.

But this is not the only reason why I am alarmed. The idea of an atheist attempting to investigate the meaning of the Bible – which is the position I am in – may look like a contradiction in terms. Devout readers are bound to find my interpretations inadequate, whatever conclusions I come to. They will miss a certain note which they consider an inseparable part of the spirit of the book; the recognition of a majesty which is higher than man, and the humility without which, they feel, its message cannot be put across. Atheist readers will also be dissatisfied, because my interpretation does not approach the subject in the usual critical way. They will have a suspicion that too many concessions have been made to the claim of belief to be absolute, without basis in reason. The historian will take exception to my lack of expert knowledge. The religious scholar will discover that I have failed to take into account some view or other which has been voiced in Biblical studies. Those readers who approach it from the angle of the history of philosophy will detect the influence of various specific schools.

But perhaps we can agree to produce something more modest, involving simply reading and re-reading the Bible and trying to reach some sort of statement – however crude and tentative – about what the Bible can mean to me as a socialist, and to the type of socialism which I have made up my mind to support; in what way it can help me to understand socialism better in its present form and as a model which we are constantly working on; and also, in what way it can stimulate our view of the world, of history, and of man. And also, of course, a statement about what I myself – precisely because I am a Marxist atheist – am capable of putting into this book, so as to increase its value for the generations to come. For it will be difficult for it to be completely forgotten, and people will scarcely ever be entirely indifferent to it.

To fulfil this modest claim is clearly an unusually ambitious venture, particularly because so far very little support is available to back up such an attempt. The situation is further complicated by the fact that the Bible has, as it were, disappeared from our cultural consciousness. So how do I begin?

2

The first part of the Bible, the Old Testament, is vast enough. And there is a good deal more to it than the part *we* know best – i.e. the story of the Creation and the lives of Adam and Eve. All that is in the book of Genesis, which is also known as the First Book of Moses. Four other books are also attributed to Moses, and these describe the fate of the children of Israel after the exodus from Egypt and their entry into the Promised Land beside the River Jordan. The annexation of territory by the twelve tribes of Jacob, the battles with the local tribes, the expansion of the Jewish people, their quarrels among themselves, their victories and defeats, the establishment of power and the formation of national independence for the Jews as they cut themselves off from the non-Jewish tribes, growing internal dissension, their downfall, signs of redemption and subjugation by the Babylonians – all this can be read in the series of books beginning with Joshua and Judges, continuing with I Kings and II Kings and I and II Chronicles down to Nehemiah, Esther and the books of the Maccabees in the Apocrypha.

The people who read these books are not necessarily critical historians, and they will not always be able to distinguish between the actual historical events and the myths and legends; but they will build up a picture of the way a community of human beings lived and struggled, and this picture will fit in with their view of history in its essentials. This feeling of an inner relationship – which has not been consciously thought out and formulated – is strengthened when they come to the Old Testament books which supplement the events described earlier, but from the spiritual angle: in the Book of Job, for instance, where they will come across the prototype of Existential despair; or in Ecclesiastes, which is attributed to the famous and mighty Solomon; in Proverbs and the Wisdom of Solomon, which collect together the experiences of a society which has had to struggle for its existence for centuries; in the Book of Psalms, which is full of beautiful poems and odes, culminating in the Song of Solomon. And even the collection of the sixteen books of the prophets who roused the Jews during the Babylonian captivity will not seem unfamiliar.

Suddenly it will not seem all that important to know which of the events described are historically true, which are mere legend devised to explain away certain facts, which parts are pure myth, and which passages represent religious views. Nor will we be interested in knowing who wrote the individual books or the exact date of composition. We will find them overflowing with life; the personal aspect is always being woven in with the social aspect, and the social aspect will permeate the personal aspect; the struggles of the great heroes will always go beyond the limits of their own personality, and the trivial quarrels of those who are merely posing as heroes will end in dishonourable defeat, because they were incapable of going beyond the limits of their own petty souls; the 'people' will not be an indeterminate mass, a tool controlled from above, but a series of individual peoples, each with its own name and its own features: the 'house of Benjamin', the 'house of Judah', 'the house of Manasseh', 'the house of Ephraim' – a people which makes its choice for good or ill, which is responsible for its own fate and is ready to bear the consequences; and finally, a people among whom a wealth of events occur – some fine, some horrible, but all fusing together in the all-embracing truth of life.

The reader who turns back to the Bible now and then and opens it at random will read and think about the possibilities inherent in his own life and in the life of the community for which he has decided to work. It seems to me that it is just this type of reading – for tradition tells us that this is how the Bible has always been read – which can testify to the indestructible values offered by the Bible, to the fact that it should be counted as one of those books which we must have read if we do not want to be poorer than other men.

3

Atheist readers may possibly interrupt me at this point to protest that the Old Testament consists of a scientifically untenable theory of how the world and man himself were created, and that materialist scientists and philosophers were kept busy for several centuries with the struggle against this theory of the creation before they succeeded in banishing it as a mere chimera. They will also allege that the theory of the creation of the world had long provided a justification for the thesis that man is at the mercy of God and of those social factors which had seized power in the name of God, in social systems in which one class did the ruling and the other class was oppressed. And that this thesis has always been an ideological tool used by reactionaries, and has helped to preserve a situation in which some people live in a state of helpless thraldom.

They will be perfectly right.

So will those who point out that the God of the Old Testament, Yahweh, or the Lord, is a tribal god, the stern, angry, cruel, vindictive image, sometimes grandiose, sometimes petty, of a tribal patriarch, or – in more objective terms – that the God of the Jews and the original Jewish religion reflects the situation in a tribal society in a state of transition between leading a nomadic life and settling down in one spot. They will continue to argue along these lines and collect a whole lot of evidence to show how the Jewish concept of God has evolved and changed . . .

They will be quite right.

But the thoughts we have voiced here have a completely different aim from ours. We are not trying to find out which elements in the Old Testament seem remote from us atheists, who have been brought up in the light of modern knowledge. The exact opposite is true; what we are trying to find out is what makes it, or could make it, seem close to us and intelligible. This type of approach compels us to look critically at the basic religious schemes outlined in the Old Testament, but on the other hand we must look equally critically at the objections raised against these schemes and consider how far they are valid. Criticisms of the theory of the creation given in the Old Testament are directed at the opening chapters of the Book of Genesis. It is true that the scientific objections are technically incontestable on objective grounds, but they are after all based on specific assumptions. This means that they cannot be turned into a form of criticism which utterly demolishes the object of the criticism.

The assumptions which underlie scientific criticism of Genesis – and this is equally true whether the criticism is on an elementary level or is of a more sophisticated nature – are always the same: the Book of Genesis simply offers one of various mythological-cum-religious descriptions of the way the world was created, and is therefore untenable when looked at from the point of view of the causal approach adopted by scientists. This type of non-religious criticism appears alongside classical science; it ties up with the views held by the ancient Greeks and Romans about a cosmic order, in which everything is provided for once and for all, encircled by geometrically exact orbits, and in which everything is consequently transparent and can be taken in at a glance – and everything that happens is inevitable. Classical scientists – from Copernicus to Newton – supplied the mathematical basis for this attitude, submitted it to proof, and modified it slightly, though they made no changes at all to the essence of the classical conception of the cosmos.

Now we are admittedly extremely surprised to find that the image of a world order advocated by the medieval Church should be basically the same as the view held by classical scientists, which would appear to run directly counter to it: both views derive from Greek thought, especially from Aristotelian philosophy.

So the struggle of the Church, which advocated a literal interpretation of Genesis, and the struggle of classical science, which refuted it – directly or indirectly – in fact were played out within the same framework of the imaginative world of classical antiquity. So we are not particularly surprised that Newton thought in terms of an initial impulse to set the cosmos in motion. In defending the traditional theory of the creation, medieval theology was thinking in terms which were as much steeped in natural theology as those of its opponent – classical science – were steeped in natural philosophy. And although later theories of evolution have made it extremely difficult to defend the traditional theory of the creation, they have not so far been able to explode it within this famework.

The point is that in the first place the Book of Genesis is definitely not a cosmogonic theory, and the causal element (to which both natural philosophy and natural theology have finally reduced the biblical stories) is of only secondary importance in the philosophical structure of the Old Testament. The whole intellectual orientation of Judaism is fundamentally different from that of classical antiquity.

Greek philosophers saw the cosmos as a causal system in which there were no discrepancies whatsoever; this system was the basis of their inner assurance, their clear, straightforward and optimistic view of the world, which imbued them with the self-confident idea that they would be capable of controlling things within this objective system. That is why classical Greek mythology is not interested in the course of history and has no feeling for it; it is full of cosmic energy. In the field of man, of personal identity, 'fate' or *moira* is the ruling element: man's achievements are subject to fate, and he can only act in the same sort of way as Odysseus, wandering between Scylla and Charybdis, unable to avoid them as they appear before him with all the static immobility of natural forces.

Jewish thinkers saw things quite differently. The Jews have never written an *Orestes*, a *Medea* or an *Electra*, and could not possibly have done so.

The statement made in Genesis is by no means primarily concerned with the genesis or creation of the world; it does not raise the question in anything like a scientific sense. The point at issue is man in a *time* system, not in a cosmic system; in a three-dimensional temporal scheme, within which everything becomes fluctuating and uncertain, and in which man must fight all the time, over and over again, to defend his existence, must make up his mind between various possibilities, choosing and rejecting, erring and being punished.

The Divine Creator of the Old Testament is far from being identical with natural theology's concept of a Prime Mover, as devised by classical antiquity, or by the Middle Ages, or by Newton. The Jew of remote antiquity, struggling to penetrate the threatening darkness which surrounded him, always found *ahead* of him events which were in fact over and done with long before, so that they could not be altered, and which contained woven within them the secret of his future. He thought of the relationship between past and future as a pivotal one. It was the exact opposite of the view held by modern man, who is brought up in the causal scientific way of thinking. So the Divine Creator always stood *in front of* him, and was at the same time the sum total of his future potential, which is wrapped in mystery, but is in fact already known and – for anyone who is high enough up to see – has long been part of the past: a past which is yet to come. The story of the creation tells us, therefore, how this human secret – man – was recorded in time. The image of the creator, the Lord, was for the Jews a revelation of man as a being who has to make decisions and act on them in a mysterious and purposeful manner, and is open-minded to the world and his fellow-men. This open-mindedness, devoid of any degree of certainty, is the exact opposite of the self-contained and well-rounded image of man held by classical antiquity. The Ancient Greek is sure of himself in everything he actively undertakes: experience teaches him that it is merely a question of *techne*, ability, skill. And yet his whole existence is uncertain: fate is always lurking in the background. The Jew, on the other hand, *knows* all the time that his position is insecure, *knows* that his existence is uncertain. That is why he takes refuge in the Lord, as the focal point on which all his potentialities converge. That is why he speaks to God, tries to talk him round, makes him promises and offers sacrifices to him, tries to enter into covenants with him – and he does all this in an attempt to discover the optimum possibilities for the security which he needs so badly. The Jew thinks of the Lord as an interpretation of man; he recognizes in him what he himself *might be*, as opposed to what he is; he also learns what he must do in order to realize this potential. An *interpretation* of this sort always reaches beyond – a little beyond at any rate – man as he actually is in his appointed position in society.

Those readers who accept the point of view I have chosen will certainly admit that the scientific objections levelled against the Book of Genesis are justified, but they will not take this too seriously. They will, in fact, grasp the point that not merely the Book of Genesis but the Old Testament as a whole contains something which is exceedingly important for the whole of European thought in general, and for contemporary socialist and Marxist thought in particular: this is the first appearance of the idea of transcendence, of a step beyond all that has so far been achieved – although it is revealed here in a pre-scientific and mythological form, it is nonetheless perfectly clear; the dream of a personal identity in the midst of Time begins to show itself here for the first time.

4

If we look at the Old Testament in this light, we soon realize that the central figure is not Adam, Abraham or Moses; nor Solomon or King David. Adam is far too blind and far too passive. The others have already been initiated into the secrets of human existence and are better or worse according to how magnanimous they are. But the figure who stands at the focal point, at the point where the crucial choice is made, is *Israel* himself or – as he is known on less solemn occasions – *Jacob*.

I will resist the temptation to tell the whole story with all its ramifications – it is in fact one of the most beautiful of the Old Testament stories, a real romance of days gone by; Thomas Mann has already retold it, and I cannot hope to emulate him. We will simply remind ourselves of the most important part of the story.

Jacob is the second son of Isaac. He knows that according to the traditional rules laid down by the Lord he has no hope of becoming a patriarch, one of the 'Great Initiators of History'.

But all the same he is reluctant to give in to the rigid impartiality of his lot. He uses every possible opportunity of changing things. He bides his time and waits. One day his brother Esau comes home from hunting absolutely famished, and he offers him a spoonful of his 'mess of pottage' in return for his birthright. For the moment this transaction does not mean much. But, Jacob tells himself, it may possibly be just the little stone which will start the avalanche rolling.

Then comes the moment when Isaac, an old man now and half blind, decides to hand over his domains. Jacob sees this as an opportunity to creep in and steal his brother's natural birthright by trickery. The risk is considerable: supposing his father sees through his imposture and pronounces an anathema which can never be removed? If he wins, he wins everything, but then if he loses, he also loses everything . . .

As Jacob hesitates, his mother intervenes. It is at her insistence that he goes to his father, trembling with fear, *to force his option – in the face of all the possibilities open to him*. He deceives his father and outwits his brother, but he takes his father's blessing with him into his long exile. He has taken advantage of his father's blindness, but he has not won. Events will soon convince him of that. He is cheated and deceived in the way he himself cheated and deceived others; and this time he is cheated in the very thing on which he has set his uneasy heart: blinded by the darkness and by passion he takes as his wife a woman he does not love, who has been slyly substituted for the woman he does love. But even now Jacob does not give up; he goes on desiring his beloved Rachel and does eventually win her. He has to serve his uncle Laban for seven years in order to win her, but when the seven years are up, seven years in which he has learnt how to become rich, he decides to return home to the place where his roots are, where he belongs. He is afraid of the scene he will have with Esau, he is afraid that he will be slain and will lose the destiny for which he has paid so dear. He is very afraid: everything is at stake. When he comes to the river which forms the frontier of his homeland, he guides his possessions and his family over the ford in the early evening and leaves them in Esau's territory, and then waits alone on the bank, safe on the other side. He is there alone to make his urgent decision.

He knows how extreme his position is: he is completely without any rights, or rather the only right he can claim was obtained under false pretences, he has received the Lord's pledge, and yet he is ambitiously determined not to lose anything. The years of blindness and of taking advantage of blindness are now behind him. And so are the nights peopled with delusions and hideously clear faces. He gave up waiting servilely for his luck to turn long ago. He takes his courage in both hands – and courage is indeed the only virtue which can take him beyond the confines of his natural destiny. He knows now what the alternatives are: he must choose between hanging on to his peaceful existence lived out in happy anonymity – and a name which might win some time from death. This is how the Book of Genesis tells of Jacob's choice:

And he rose up that night, and took his two wives, and his two women servants, and his eleven sons, and passed over the ford Jabbok. And he took them, and sent them over the brook, and sent over that he had. And Jacob was left alone; and there wrestled a man with him until the breaking of the day. And when he saw that he prevailed not against him, he touched the hollow of his thigh; and the hollow of Jacob's thigh was out of joint as he wrestled with him. And he said, Let me go, for the day breaketh. And he said, I will not let thee go, except thou bless me. And he said unto him, What is thy name? And he said, Jacob. And he said, Thy name shall be called no more Jacob, but Israel [he who fought with God]: for as a prince hast thou power with God and with men, and hast prevailed. And Jacob asked him, and said, Tell me, I pray thee, thy name. And he said, Wherefore is it that thou dost ask after my name? And he blessed him there.   (Genesis xxxii, 22–9)

I feel that this scene provides the key to an understanding of the Old Testament; it tells how man becomes a subject, a person. Adam, whom God *created* from a lump of clay, was not an individual person. Adam is not even a proper human *name*, but a label denoting a whole species, mankind in general. And Eve merely denotes the division into two different sexes. From the point of view of personal identity 'Adam and Eve' are merely neuter: they are a specific entity, it is true, but they are not real people yet.

Jacob is utterly different. He sets little store by promises, and does not believe in gifts. He knows that anything offered as a gift is the result of chance. He disregards his natural destiny and is determined to override it by means of his own actions. By making a choice which goes beyond the possibilities open to him, he emerges from the general run of his race and wins himself an individual name and a series of individual features. His action is the first action to have any sort of historical status, it is the first authentic human action. Israel becomes the *Lord of Time*.

We should also note that Jacob's transcendence of his own boundaries is majestically monistic and all of a piece. The choice he makes, the state of affairs which he sets down, was not 're-corded' in advance in the Lord's decree. Nowhere in the story of Jacob, nor anywhere else in the Old Testament for that matter, does the Lord stamp a pattern known in advance on to material which is as yet completely without form or identity, which is how the classical world and, under its influence, medieval theology, together with classical science, interpreted things, in dualistic terms. ...

Man 'is elected' provided that he comes to a decision, chooses freely and confirms his choice by his actions.

If there is still a note of dualism in this transcendence, it is a minute amount, which we can easily ignore since it is the expression of its age, establishing something which is constantly moving forwards, dynamically orientated towards the sum of authentic potentialities possessed by the community of man from the very first.

But this idea which is so fundamental to the Old Testament – the idea of choice and personal identity – and which is exemplified by Israel and its twelve tribes in all their manifold variety, is basically quite different from the classical idea of a predestined system and a cosmic harmony. God's 'chosen people' are given nothing at the outset, and are granted no special exemptions. First of all, the system must be created, the Promised Land must be wrested from their enemies. The outcome of any decision is always in doubt. And when the Old Testament commanders take counsel with the Lord before the decisive battle, they are simply making a realistic appraisal of their own prospects which will form part of the basis of their decision, as in Jacob's struggle. The children of Israel are never quite sure whether their decisions will even prove to be lasting. They are always being made aware of how precarious and dramatic their beginnings are, and in spite of this, or perhaps because of it, they allow all their actions to be guided by their consciousness of the infinite possibilities which lie within them and represent their secret hopes; by their actions they break open this potential as if it were the mysterious womb of a woman who is to give birth for the first time and produce something new; something which can never be reproduced, and yet is bound up with all that has gone before, and at the same time represents the fountain from which their future destiny will spurt forth. That is why the Lord commands that Israel should sacrifice a male animal and 'all that openeth the womb' (Exodus xxxiv, 19). This also explains why the Jews in the Old Testament set such store by sexuality, and why the Jewish Bible contains so many beautiful love-stories. Sex opens up the womb of the future and places in it a seed which contains a complete record of the past, as a threat, an example and a warning. So man recreates everything which is already written, with the idea of refashioning it in his own image. He is constantly risking his whole existence. He is the demiurge of his own fate, and he knows it.

5

Choice and personal identity . . .

But isn't this attempt at an interpretation really rather fantastic? Doesn't it involve jettisoning all the fundamental Marxist criteria? Isn't it a subjectivist distortion of the Marxist concept of history? Isn't it really a fervent – over-fervent in fact – apologia for the Bible? All these questions are perfectly in order. It is clearly essential that I should make my attempt credible.

Marx was an atheist. But he was never the sort of primitive atheist who would not have asked himself what statement about man as a social being is involved in any specific concept of God.

He was neither a natural philosopher nor a classical materialist. He devised the concept of a practical philosophy, of epoch-making actions by means of which the man who is hampered by limits – a whole social class – can overstep his boundaries and can throw his whole weight into this action which will change the world.

And finally – why try to avoid the issue? – Marx was born into a Jewish family. It is true that he was miles away from orthodox Jewish religiosity, but in his innermost heart he carried the individual experiences gleaned over thousands of years by the Jewish people, who believed in what was promised to them. He carries within him genes which stir up in him a feeling for Time as it was given to man. I am convinced that Marx was more capable than virtually anyone before him of reading the prophecies given in the Bible. If not, he would scarcely have created such a majestically monistic philosophy.

Yes – if we think about Marxism systematically, Marx's materialism becomes questionable in the extreme.

2

JESUS
Man and Miracle

1

Christianity is all about Jesus Christ. For Christians, Jesus, Son of God and Son of Man, is both a three-in-one God and a unique man.

He causes the theologians a lot of trouble.

But what do Marxists see him as? What can the religious concept of Christ mean for Marxist atheism?

We are now two thousand years away from the period which is known as the 'time of Christ'. Over these two thousand years Jesus has lived on in the minds of whole nations; for long periods he is their unqualified leader, but then his image becomes confused, giving way to a certain extent to other gods, to other ideas, fetishes and myths; but it never quite disappears altogether. The long history of the Christian faith boasts a large number of occasions when people have tried to come to grips with this mysterious and ambiguous figure, to interpret him, both for themselves and for others.

What induced all these people, some unimportant, some important, to undertake such an exacting task? How did the vision of Christ manage to fire their imagination? Why did they try to fit this fading image into the pattern of their own existence?

The Enlightenment explained this by accusing the previous centuries of deliberately bolstering up obscure cults and an ideology which was totally unauthenticated from every point of view; but we cannot be content with this answer. Even if we allow the argument to stand, we are still left with the problem of how such deceit was possible, or what sort of response the idea of Christ found in the life of ordinary men and women, why it could find an echo in men's hearts – which is what really did happen in various different periods and situations.

34

So what do we make of all the various interpretations which have been recorded down the ages? Which of them should be thought of as authentic, or at any rate as having done what they set out to do? And what sort of criteria should we judge them by, anyway?

Can we banish this old/new legend to the realm of pure fantasy, judging it as fantastic because we cannot manage to tell it to our children as a bedtime story? Or would we rather think of Jesus in terms of his human form, as he appears in folk-tales and popular drama – carved wooden cribs with a tinfoil star over the manger, the nativity play from the Riesengebirge, in which the Devil has the same limp as the local veteran and the executioner's legs are as bandy as a country fireman's? But is this type of interpretation really any good? and should we stick to it when we come across a parallel version which is thoroughly distorted, full of horror, full of darting flames, full of religious mania and mass hysteria, full of the most melancholy delusions imagined by a mind inflamed by passion, full of ecstasy reached by flagellation, and bigoted raving? Or should we perhaps leave the whole business to the theologians – only to shrug our shoulders in an arrogant fashion at hair-splitting scholars discussing God's name and attributes and at the learned disputes about whether Christ was god or man? Shall we instead join in the scientific arguments about Jesus as a historical phenomenon? Or shall we agree with those who point out that from the strictly scientific point of view there is no evidence to prove that Jesus did not exist? Or with the adherents of a positivistic method of writing history, who put forward the opposite argument, i.e. that there is no conclusive evidence that he *did* exist? Shall we intervene in the quarrel about whether certain passages in Josephus or Tacitus are authentic, thus condemning ourselves to flounder in the quagmire of never-ending quarrels in which dilettantism and emotion emerge triumphant? From the point of view of Marxism, all this merely proves that some people believe in Jesus and some don't. It also raises the question of the social and personal situation in which the believers and the non-believers find themselves, and of the motivation behind their actions. Quite apart from the question of whether or not Jesus was a historical figure, belief in him is a historical fact which must be recognized over the heads of all the squabblers. Jesus exists as an absolutely specific and momentous structure within the minds of men, which has taken on a whole range of different forms, shapes, and patterns during the two thousand years of its existence. And Marxists, who are always eager to get down to the root of things, will probably do their best to trace the original model from which all the others have developed. This is the only way they can obtain some sort of yardstick, not merely an extrinsic one, but one which is appropriate to the matter in hand; this criterion will give them the opportunity of recognizing and judging the versions which are wide of the mark, so that they will be able to establish what the original Christian motivation was and what the real significance of Christianity is: what message does it bring to the centuries that followed its coming? what is this 'New Law'? what exactly is the 'Word of God'? what is the *Evangelion*, compared to the view of the world held by the Jews and the ancient Greeks?

If we look at things in this way, we can understand Jesus without becoming religious ourselves and without having to decide whether or not he existed. In that case he will not enter our consciousness as a cult object or as a figure to whom we pray, but as one of the models for human life, which during the course of history emerged as a new answer to the basic questions, as an alternative to the old and obsolete answers; the answer he put forward was so profound that it still has something to say to us today and to teach us – in spite of the number of times it has been distorted over the two thousand years since it first appeared, and in spite of all those occasions when it has been 'definitively' refuted.

2

The New Testament canon contains four Gospels. Each contains different versions of stories concerned with the life of Jesus, beginning with his birth, continuing to his death, and beyond it to his 'Ascension'. If we put these four texts together, the result will be a Gospel 'synopsis' with the gaps in the individual accounts filled in from the information given in the others. The Acts of the Apostles carry on from the Gospels, being a description of what happened to

certain young followers of Jesus who continued to spread his doctrines, and of how individual Churches or Christian communities
came into being. These are the people to whom the Epistles are
addressed: the letters from the apostles or other leading representatives of the new movement who were eager to co-ordinate and
develop it. And lastly, the canon also includes the Apocalypse,
which is a sort of prophetic vision and is also known as the Revelation of St John.

Vast quantities of theological literature have been based on this
relatively modest amount of material. Historical and critical research into the New Testament also deals with these same books.

It would be quite impossible to quote even a fraction of the
conclusions reached by research into the New Testament, which has
attained absolutely vast proportions today. At any rate there is no
question of doing so here. We have something different in mind: the
point of our survey is to dig right down to the roots of Christianity,
establishing what it wanted to achieve in its own era and what it
did achieve; or in other words, our aim is to understand its significance by close reference to the religion itself, from within, as it
were, and to compare it to our own spiritual orientation.

In that case it is patently obvious that the usual procedure used
by atheists during the Enlightenment is not particularly relevant.
It was used at that period to demonstrate that the Gospels were
not authentic and were positively two-faced, the method being to
take individual thoughts, maxims or parables out of context and
compare and contrast them; a rider was added pointing out that
everyone could select whatever he felt like from the Holy Scriptures
for every conceivable occasion. It is true that the Christian apolo-
gists frequently used the same method, but that is no reason for
thinking of the Holy Scriptures as a type of sophistic literature.
This type of machination merely shows that Christianity was acting beneath itself when it used this method. The fact that statements which really do contradict each other can be found in the
Bible merely proves that the Gospels are made up of a number of
different historical layers, and that we must differentiate between
them if we want to establish the approximate date when they were
written and ask ourselves which passages represent the actual,

original Christian mission and which parts are later interpretations.

The foundations of the problem were laid by scientific and historical research, the results of which even the theologians have been forced to treat with respect. But it is only in the last few decades, and indeed in the last few years, when Christ's message has sounded less and less credible to modern men and women and has lost a good deal of its urgency, that they have been forced to reflect seriously on the question of what exactly Christ's message is. Both Protestant and Roman Catholic theologians have set out to remove the mythological element from the texts of the canon (though the Catholics have been considerably more hesitant and cautious than the Protestants). They have produced some remarkable results, which open up a whole series of possibilities – predominantly practical ones. We will be coming back to this later.

As for the argument about whether the results produced by theological research have anything to do with genuine belief, we will leave that to the theologians; we are not qualified to join in.

When Marxists study history, they cannot understand it in the same way as they understand natural events. The laws of history are not of the same order as the laws of nature. They are laws created by human subjectiveness, by man's practical faculty for making things concrete. Any element of history which appears to be dead (over and done with, completed), in other words any event which is 'past', is really weighed down with a series of challenges, and becomes an inspiration in practical terms for new action. It is a driving force which lies hidden outside us, underlying our conscious impulses. So if we study history seriously, we can never be unprejudiced observers, since we are always personally involved. We are anxious to discover beneath the surface of what appears to be a historical reality the challenge which men now dead recorded there when they were alive and fighting. According to whether we accept this challenge (appropriately or inappropriately) we then build up our own prototypes for the world of man, and offer our lives in an effort to translate these prototypes into reality; we thus become living and creative histories ourselves, full of actual events. When we come up against the past we always find ourselves faced with the question of what we really want; the past forces us to be stricter about our unprincipled subjective desires, to be more sharply critical in building up our own historical schemes, to feel a greater sense of responsibility in everything that we, as social beings, undertake.

If we look at it this way, Jesus may not seem to be a figure whose existence is historically proven. This does not mean of course that we want to side with those who insist that he never existed. We are simply not interested. Jesus exists for us in a much more positive form: as an embodiment of a symbol, a symbol for a specifically Jewish way of looking at the world and at mankind; this attitude first crops up in the world of Judaism and in the classical world at the beginning of our era, then spreads and moves beyond the narrow horizons of its national identity. If we understand Jesus in this light, we are free to reflect on him as a Gospel figure and on the contents of the challenge which he embodies and brings to us.

Christ's challenge questions our subjectiveness, our plans, our schemes, our practical activity. So our answer must consist of something more than a mere 'refutation' of the legend; nor is it enough to say that we don't believe in God or in Jesus's divinity, that we are atheists. In fact the questions raised by the original version of Christianity are not of a religious nature. We cannot get to the real answer until we acknowledge in no uncertain terms that these questions do have a historical justification, in that they attempt to express a scale of importance which emerges from the activity of men as social beings in history. Giving a satisfactory answer to these questions has nothing to do with theory, with careful deliberation, with words, but is, in the last analysis, a practical matter.

Now what exactly are these questions?

3

Jesus was a Jew. He was killed by Jews. He rose again from the dead and ascended into Heaven.

This is the basic Gospel message.

Jesus was a Jew: the Old Testament idea of 'choosing' had

exactly the same importance for him as for any other Jew. He was clearly an educated Jew who knew his Old Testament and was steeped in its spirit.

But he lived in a period when the Jewish people, the children of Israel, once a tightly knit community completely separate from the other tribes, began to break up; this dissolution went hand in hand with the increasing universality of the links between countries and nations within the Roman Empire, which meant that the fate of one group of people reduced to slavery became the fate of everybody.

Jesus is a Jew both from the objective point of view, i.e. by birth, and from the subjective point of view, i.e. in the light of his outlook on life and his actions. Initially, his message was not intended for the world and mankind as a whole. It was not *planned* as a universal message; though this does not mean that it does not contain the seeds of this type of universality. But Jesus addresses his message exclusively to the Jews, to God's chosen people – in the strict sense of the term, as it is found in Israel/Jacob. Jesus is one of a long series of prophets who observe with distaste, and bitterness – and later on with hatred and menace – the gradual decline of that direct experience of God in their contemporaries which always occurred in the tension between choice and election, decision and liberating action which was demanded of them at any one specific time.

The Old Testament is transformed into a transcendental theology – in many cases under the influence of foreign (Greek and Oriental) elements; the Lord ceases to represent a temporal call for decisive action and becomes an *object* which can be tested and subjected to analysis, then later honoured and revered. The world, which was initially an undivided whole, representing a harmonious union of subject and object, now disintegrates into two separate realms, subject and object, heaven and earth; men would like to get away from their divided state and recreate total unity by their actions, but they are dismembered into two conflicting 'substances', body and soul, so that there is a total dichotomy, with no means of making the transition from one to the other.

That was the situation when Jesus made his appearance with his call to action. If we read the Gospels carefully we cannot fail to

notice that his attitude towards this type of dogmatic interpretation of the Old Testament is one of scorn, even of hatred. He is
always getting into arguments with the official representatives of
the faith – with the learned leaders and the men who interpret the
law, the Pharisees and the priests; he is always denouncing them in
public. Unlike them, he rejects the dogmatism of the Old Testament, and then tackles their narrow-minded adherence to questions
of second-rate or even third-rate importance, to every possible type
of ritualistic regulation concerning such matters as purification; he
sees all these as nothing but obstacles to a thorough understanding
of the inspiration provided by the Old Testament. That is why he is
not concerned with developing some new system of teaching, a new
theology, a religious or ethical system based on merit. He cannot be
concerned with this type of thing. We absolutely agree with the
Protestant theologians who hold the view that it is wrong to search
for some new theology or a new anthropological attitude in Jesus's
original doctrine. They consider that Jesus is not preaching a new
moral or humanistic ideal, nor listing the qualities which charac-
terize a 'devout' man, i.e. a man who has developed harmoniously.
Instead they point out that all these theories are completely alien
to the Jewish spirit, and belong to the thinking of the ancient
Greeks and Romans.

Everything points to the fact that Jesus's concern was to lead the
people of Israel back to their original faith, to that certainty in
which the Lord was continually with them as a challenge to his
chosen people – to those who have to decide, to choose, and who
must throw themselves wholeheartedly into this act of choosing.
He was concerned with bringing about the reappearance of that
Israel for whom the whole future was a matter of decision here and
now; with the appearance of that dynamic process of progress and
transcendence which brings back what should have been there from
the very beginning – the Promised Land, the 'Kingdom of God'.
Jesus inevitably seemed to the Pharisees and high priests to be
attacking the Law of Moses; to be disdaining all those elements
which, according to them, formally affirmed the Law – rites, regulations and rules concerning sacrifices. These things lay in their
power and indeed actually *stemmed from their power*. Jesus de-

fended himself with the words: 'I came not to destroy [the Law], but to fulfil it.' But, needless to say, this defence did not help his case at all.

We must emphasize once more – and anyway it follows on from our interpretation of Jesus – that he did not appear suddenly, as an individual phenomenon. At the time there was a whole series of people who held the same spiritual attitude; they formed a variety of more or less radical sects and were generally known as 'prophets'; in other words, they were people who were able to detect the seeds of recovery and the narrow paths leading to a possible way out of the unhappy situation in which the children of Israel found themselves at that point; i.e. they spoke of potential 'means of salvation'.

Jesus directed most of his efforts towards the people whose simple faith seemed to him to offer the best hope of bringing the children of Israel to their senses: simple fishermen, vine-dressers, craftsmen, the poor, and the homely, care-worn Jewish women. All this weighed against him in the eyes of the representatives of the orthodox Jewish religion. Jesus is quite clearly a Jew of his own time. He knows that there is not much room for a chosen people in a world which is falling under the increasingly powerful yoke of the heathen; that the situation is narrowing down to the final critical either/or. It is Jacob's dilemma all over again; the decisive choice cannot be put off any longer; it may be too late 'by to-morrow'; the Promised Land, the 'Kingdom of Heaven' is at hand. So the whole of the future is projected forward into the present moment, into 'today'. The decision must be reached *today*. The choice must be made *today*. Either for God and for Jesus, who is God's prophet; or against them. The man who makes the choice chooses at a single stroke the whole of the future, salvation or damnation. So it is not a matter of any old decision much like any other, but of a definitive decision, once and for all. Thus everything that Jesus says comes down to a demand for a *radical* decision, which must be made in the knowledge that everything depends on it. We must enter into it totally, with our whole being.

That is why Jesus's mission involves calling on both friends and enemies. But whereas his friends are uncertain and vacillating –

after all they are people with ordinary everyday worries on their minds and Jesus does ask a good deal of them, everything in fact! – his enemies are unanimous, determined and obstinate. It is easy to predict what Jesus's fate will be.

Are we to think of Jesus as a social revolutionary? The answer will obviously depend on how his programme looks, and on the content of his message. Jesus stirs up the masses of Judaism, urging them to take a radical decision in favour of the Kingdom of God, which is at hand.

But what does Jesus mean by the Kingdom of God? It would be only too easy to find in the Gospels an outline for a social order governed by social justice, a social-cum-political scheme which Jesus is doing his best to put into practice. If we look at things in this light, the arguments which put forward the theory that Jesus was 'actually' the first Communist, that he was concerned with social justice, and that Marxism is – if thought out to its logical conclusion – 'actually' a secularized version of Christianity seem to us naïve. This type of interpretation is inept and glosses over the real heart of the matter. If we want to get at least an approximate idea of what Jesus meant by the Kingdom of God, we must leave the Gospels and turn to the Apocalypse or Revelation of St John, which belongs to the latest group of New Testament writings.

Using very sombre images and symbols wrapped up in a series of complicated ciphers, the author of the Apocalypse complains that Israel's position, the position of the 'holy ones' who have fallen into the hands of the 'beast of prey' (the 'city' or the 'harlot'), cannot be maintained in the distant future. His most violent condemnation is directed at Rome, and he rejects the city entirely, with much bitterness and hatred. But so far as we can see, the strong protest which he levels against the might of Rome does not stem merely from some sort of political consideration or from the urge to bring immediate pressure to bear on the situation. He is much more concerned about the fact that 'Rome' – 'the Heathen' – appears to be threatening the very heart of Israel, that part of it which is the innermost guarantee that it will continue to exist as an independent entity, the element which Jesus and his followers rescued from the long Old Testament tradition as the prerequisite for an existence worthy of a human being. The spirit of classical antiquity, which had degenerated into Hellenism by then anyway, was completely alien to *these* particular Jews, and they would not have been able to live in such a society. Hellenism represented an outlook in which there was no room for freedom of choice, or in other words for that element which constitutes the dignity of man (it must be admitted that this idea would have been too abstract for the Jews of that period). The classical attitude also lacked – indeed this was its most important drawback – the possibility for free development of one's own free will. The Jews who lived in the time of Christ were miles away from the classical concept of God as an object, and the idea of representing him pictorially was to them both offensive and meaningless; they even called it 'blasphemy'. Worshipping objects, images and pillars was to them the equivalent of fornicating.

So in demanding that a stand should be made against Rome, the writer of the Apocalypse was not fired by any idea of social justice. Nor did his challenge lead to the Utopian concept of a new social order. Had this been the case, had Christianity found its deepest motivation in such a concept, it would scarcely have outlived its own era.

No! We can see that something much deeper and much more fundamental was at stake: a blue-print for a type of life which demands of man a responsible decision, which he must stick to by waging a remorseless inner struggle which pierces him down to his very roots; but at the same time opens the door to a new future in which man is more than he was before. But the Jews who lived in the time of Christ did not see this as a method of achieving personal perfection or some sort of 'moral development', as a method which one could use on one's own, independently of other people, without reference to time or place. The decision is made by Israel, by men as a community. The outcome is never solely a question of personal advantage – this idea would have been alien and unacceptable to the Old Testament Jews – but of the advantage of a sharply defined community, which can now develop further and become still more concrete. The misfortune of one individual, or even his death, does not result in horror or emptiness, but in an enriched and deeper degree of reality. The decadent idea of individual salvation, and of leading the sort of virtuous life by which one bribes one's way to a celestial place in the sun and is filled with panic at the idea of death, is utterly and completely foreign to Judaism in the time of Christ; and this can be equated with early Christianity.

The Apocalypse speaks out accordingly against the Greek or 'heathen' view of the world and of life, and predicts its downfall. It declares that its outlook is incompatible with the outlook of the cultures which think that the cosmos of man's potential is sealed. The Apocalypse contrasts this fornicating world with the 'new Jerusalem' in which 'God shall wipe away all tears from their eyes; and there shall be no more death . . .' (Revelation XXI, 4). The writer 'saw no temple therein' to separate men from God, but saw instead man himself, who alone hears the call to action and is ready to make his choice. So the Apocalypse dies away in an eschatology, waiting in hope for the end, for the last things, which shall also be the first. The idea of the Last Judgement and of justice being done has not yet become a cosmic catastrophe to be played out in the dim distant future. The Judgement is made here and now, immediately. As soon as we have grasped the fact that the downfall of the harlot is inevitable once sentence has been passed against her, everything is over for us. A verdict has been pronounced, and it can never be reversed. Man has decided in favour of the new Jerusalem and has put his whole being into his choice, down to the last shiver of his soul. The actions which provide the sequel are motivated by this choice.

Eschatological thinking is characteristic of apocalyptical Christianity. It addresses itself directly to the future, in which a decision is to be made about man's existence. This situation gives it a sort of shock, but a shock which is nevertheless full of hope; everything hangs in the balance and men can make their secret conditions in the face of this situation. For that is the lot of all men and, inextricably bound up with this, the lot of the community as a whole and therefore man's personal lot as well.

Man comes to a decision, and by doing so crosses over the river of Time.

4

If we project the vision described in the Apocalypse back into the time of Jesus, it becomes clear that we can scarcely think of Jesus as a social reformer, or even as a revolutionary in the normal sense of the word. We will not find any traces whatsoever of a programme of social reform in the Gospels, unless of course we follow the thoroughly primitive method of trying to piece one together by taking individual passages out of context. It is up to the theologians to argue about whether Jesus did actually think of himself as the son of God. The picture we have built up of his character compels us to doubt it. On the other hand, it is virtually certain that the Jews who were carried away by his message and actions did see him as the Messiah; and during a certain phase of his career truly fantastic efforts were made to turn him into the King of the Jews. Jewish Messianism was the product of Israel's long-standing tradition of fighting battles, the outcome of which was not always successful by any means; and it grew stronger as their national unity progressively disintegrated, leading eventually to centuries of subjection. During the Roman occupation their yearning increased, and in the first century A.D. – a period full of tragedy for the Jewish people – this longing fastened on to the legendary figure of Jesus. This was definitely the beginning of the religious cult.

Obviously there was no trace of such a cult while Jesus was still alive and moving about among the people. Or at any rate, there was no cult connected with him personally. It is true that he was thought of as a prophet, a saviour, perhaps even as a king; in other words, he was seen as an extraordinary and electrifying figure, but not as a god. His actions took on a sort of halo. They were unique, they had never been seen before and could never be repeated, they were miraculous. So Jesus 'performed miracles'. The stories told of him by the Evangelists are primitive in the extreme, as is the carefully upheld tradition about his miracles.

And yet – Jesus did perform miracles! If we really soak ourselves in the various accounts with genuine sympathy and understanding, taking into account the descriptions of the attendant circumstances, we can see that all the miracles attributed to him serve as patterns, and are intended to make us consider all that is most vital in the universe.

All the miracles described in the Gospels have one thing in common: they interfere with the causality which governs nature, with the chain reaction of cause and effect which controls the world of objects. The result is disconcerting, in fact positively ... miraculous! We should also notice one other important point, which is common to every account of this type: Jesus never performs his miracles with the intention of scaring his audience by his supernatural powers or of emphasizing that he was sent by God. Rather the reverse: the miracles are always somehow incidental, hesitant. It almost looks as if he is rather unwilling to perform them at all. This is typical of his miracles. So what is it that *really* interferes with the causal pattern of nature? What is it that changes in such a disconcerting fashion the tediously rigid pattern of development in the external world? There can be no doubt about the answer: it is the action, the subjective action which imprints a new order, a new law on to the chain of cause and effect, forcing it to aim towards a specific goal and to translate itself into reality along those lines.

But Jesus has another far-reaching view of what a miracle is: according to this, a miracle is not a trivial decision just like any other, an arbitrary act which benefits somebody; it is the radical answer to an urgent summons, an action which can only be accomplished if our whole personality – everything we are and possess – is brought into play; for this is the only way we can possibly make that crucial step which takes us beyond limits that have never been surpassed before.

The miracle transcends everything that is trivial, banal, ordinary, 'natural', 'normal'. What happens is unique, entailing absolute self-realization. And so Jesus's miracles teach us more about the *essence* of an action which has a historical effect than we can learn from boring descriptions of the exploits of the heroes of the classical world.

By performing his miracles, Jesus shows the sceptical members of his Jewish audience – people who have never taken the slightest risk, who would never in their wildest dreams have thought such a thing possible – that the 'natural course of things' really can be radically interfered with, and that man is capable of performing miracles.

Of course he does also show that this can only happen provided that certain requirements are fulfilled. He lists a whole series of prerequisites of this type on various occasions, though in the end they boil down to one basic one: the 'law' of *love*. This golden rule of Christianity has been misinterpreted by later periods, along with everything else. And, again along with everything else that was new in Jesus's message, it has frequently been misused by those in authority, to their own advantage. In this falsified form, as an 'all-embracing' love, all-forgiving, classless and abstract, it has been severely criticized, and rightly so. And yet love is one of those eternal themes where it is extremely important to understand what it originally meant in Jesus's own time. For it does not have even the minutest trace of sentimentality, it has nothing to do with bewitching our senses and our emotions, it does not contain any sort of moral instruction intended to teach us to put into practice certain absolute values within an abstract moral system, nor does it proclaim a feeble pacifism. In fact Jesus's mission has nothing to do with demanding specific and concrete virtues of us – chastity, poverty and obedience, for example. He doesn't draw up a specific moral code. He doesn't prescribe certain duties regardless, without taking the circumstances into account: for instance, he doesn't think of marriage as indissoluble, and he doesn't say that wealth or poverty as such are necessarily a good thing. Any reference he does make to specific 'virtues' is merely a repetition of Moses's instructions – and the Jews were already very familiar with these.

The heart of the matter is to be found elsewhere. Jesus is convinced that before we can come to a radical decision, before we can achieve a 'miracle', we must be filled with love: we must be aware – steeped in the sort of profound knowledge that governs our whole being and is sometimes felt with total immediacy – that we only *exist* when we surpass ourselves: in our own eyes, in the eyes of our fellow-men, and in the eyes of God; and when we know that this act of transcendence challenges our minds, our strength of purpose, our passion – both in the active and passive sense – and demands that we should bring all our senses into play. That being so, we do not need any instructions about what concrete action we should take in any given circumstances: whether we should share out our riches or keep them for ourselves, whether we should desert our wives or stick to them, whether we should kill our rivals or let them off.

If we think out Jesus's concept of love to its radical conclusion, we will see that it always involves a confrontation with death. But if love is present in the form of a passionate desire for life on a more elevated level – and that is the essence of Jesus's appeal – death cannot win (not only physical death, but death in a thousand trivial shapes and forms). That is why love is both the most difficult state for us to achieve and the most elevated; its diametrical opposite being the fear of death. Surpassing this limit involves 'rising from the dead' or 'living as a man'. This means that everything is easy, even those things which are totally impossible. Once we have reached this point, they are miracles no longer, since everything seems perfectly natural. The only people who think of them as miraculous are those who have not made the decisive step.

So Jesus's preaching does not tell us to love everybody. He doesn't tell us what to do in every single situation. All he asks of us is that we should enter into the situation wholeheartedly. And his own actions show us that it really is possible: man is capable of performing miracles. Miracles are performed. They are the nodal points in the web of history, the junctures where something unique takes place, an incident which can never be repeated. And if we look at it this way, love turns out to be the radically subjective element of history.

Why be afraid of this type of miracle?

Why not wish for one instead?

5

When Jesus put forward his radical doctrine about making decisions, about the Kingdom of God and about love, he was not thinking of 'mankind pure and simple'. He was not formulating the basic principles of some sort of 'new humanism'. It would be utterly wrong to think that that was what he had in mind. Humanism dates from a good deal later. Jesus had in mind no one but the Jews of his own time, the Jews of Israel: so in this sense the original version of Christianity, the version which goes right back to Jesus himself, or, if you like, the version presented in the Apocalypse, cannot be called humanistic, unless we choose to understand the concept of humanism in non-historical terms. It therefore seems wrong to me that either the Christian camp or the Marxist camp should think of Christianity as a form of humanism. It will be much more relevant to look into the connection between Christianity and humanism – by which I always mean Christianity in the time of Christ.

The version of Christianity given in the Apocalypse registers several closely connected protests: it protests against the poverty of the dogmatic theology of the Old Testament, because it has betrayed and buried alive the inherent strength of Israel, which is man's decision freely to perform an action which transcends his own limits: against 'paganism', both in its Oriental form (which is attacked particularly fiercely in the books attributed to Moses and in the books of the prophets) and in its classical form, which dates from the period of Roman expansion. The pagans of this last period in particular turned out to be extremely dangerous from the subjective point of view – i.e. from the point of view of Israel – because they threatened the children of Israel with the loss of their identity, without which the Jews could not continue to live as a chosen people, and indeed could not exist at all.

But the Roman world, with its ideas about order and its practical use of power, was itself already in decline; the great days of the classical conception of the world, as expressed by Homer, then by the pre-Socratics and Plato, right down to Aristotle, were over. Their mythical archetype, which the Greek philosophers later illuminated by the light of their reason, is familiar with the idea of a cosmic order and an all-embracing harmony, in which everything has its own appointed place. The world is seen as a place in which men can find their way about relatively easily and can develop their *techne*, or skills, using them to gain gradual mastery over the forces of nature and over objects. Man finds his way outwards from within. He has no idea of what it means to take history into account in his deliberations. He just watches time passing, noticing the way it acts in cycles; but he is not keyed to the future, and looks back at the past instead, seeing it always in static terms as a 'golden age'. This spiritual ambience gave rise to the rational analysis of science, to the 'scientific' attitude which thinks in terms of objects, and to an interest in technology as a means of gaining mastery over the world.

This brilliant legacy of the classical world was already crumbling swiftly away in the time of Christ: its basic ideas were distorted by constant repetition and the infiltration of foreign elements from eastern religions and from superstition. The pure spirit of the classical world was replaced by Hellenistic eclecticism, and all types of skills were abused over and over again. It is true that Rome was still powerful in the political and military fields; she was still fully in control of the cosmos of her own empire; but the smell of decay was already wafting out from the upper ranks.

The original tendencies of the Jews ran counter to those of the classical world. At the time of Christ's birth they came together. And although Jesus's new, radical message, his law of love, was not intended for export, but was simply meant for home consumption by the children of Israel, his doctrine was nevertheless used to bury the decaying corpse. The Jewish people suffered defeat. But their radical conception of the world – Christianity – emerged victorious. This is perfectly logical: when the debacle of the original classical outlook had revealed its weaknesses, an attitude which pointed out that the essence of all questions was 'What is man?' could not fail to win the day.

The answer went like this: if we do not know what man is, then there is no point in being in control of nature. Man is a creature who evolves by fighting and by answering the call of the present with a free decision. If he manages to love in a radical manner, he breaks open the womb of the future by his own action, and thus surpasses his potential. That is his whole secret, that is what makes him a miracle in himself; something which is there and cannot be reproduced.

We have here the antithesis of the humanism which was linked several centuries later to the classical view of the world and of man. It is the concept of *Hominism*.

The cry of *'Ecce homo!'* – 'See what a man this is!' – which echoes down to us from the time of Christ, provides a definition of early Christianity and is an original Christian challenge.

The conflict between humanism and hominism drags on in the following centuries. It is the most burning problem we have to face today.

3

ST AUGUSTINE

Passion and Death

1

Aurelius Augustinus, Bishop of Hippo, lived from A.D. 354 to 430, shortly after Christianity had become an acknowledged religion receiving official support, right in the middle of an age when the last pillars of the Roman Empire – once so glorious – collapsed under the pressure of Vandal raids and attacks by other freebooters. He counts as one of the greatest of the Fathers in the history of the Church and in every description of Christian philosophy he is seen as the central figure in the work of the Fathers of the Church. Some modern, Existentially orientated Christian philosophers turn to him as a figure whom they can call on in their intensive experience of God. And contemporary philosophical anthropologists, both the bourgeois ones, and, occasionally, the Marxist ones, find that the problems with which they are so systematically concerned are raised, and indeed solved, by St Augustine.

But what makes St Augustine really interesting to us today?

2

When St Augustine wrote his *Confessions*, he was already an important representative of a powerful Church. They are extraordinary for a number of reasons. They have often been interpreted. This spirited autobiography has many grateful readers, who see it as an introduction to Augustine's philosophical and theological work. It is probably of crucial importance for the aims we have in mind in this study.

The thirteen books of St Augustine's *Confessions* are far more than a critical portrayal of his own life; even their immediate objective, which was to defend their author against malicious enemies of the Church, inevitably led to strongly self-centred definitions: he gives his readers a picture of the process of conversion as it worked on him personally, of the transition from non-belief to belief, from a life far removed from God to a life filled with God; a struggle with fate ending in a final catharsis.

This literary transformation is much more relevant for us today than the sober biographical facts.

We shall now describe this conflict.

The *Confessions* describe in a highly dramatic way how man as an individual can cross the threshold of his own death. The anti-thetical concepts 'I/death' are brought into the picture at the very beginning, where Augustine tells of an incident which occurred when he was suffering from some illness as a child. This is quickly superseded, it is true, by the impetuous arrival of the young North African in the lively city of Carthage. Friends, the theatre, school, women, successes – he is totally caught up in the colourful and varied life of the town. The death of his father is a shock, but a purely external one: he is forced to live on a more modest scale, with fewer amusements, and to devote more time to his studies. Then a copy of Cicero's *Hortensius* comes his way. This has a very violent influence on him: '. . . All my empty dreams suddenly lost their charm and my heart began to throb with a bewildering passion for the wisdom of eternal truth.' [1]

From this moment boredom, disappointment and increasing bitterness dog Augustine's footsteps. He knows that this is still a muddled state which does not yet lead automatically to the type of experience that we should now call 'Existential'. What is needed is a real jolt to radicalize the conflict and reveal with drastic clarity what Augustine thinks at the time is thorough boredom with life in general. Augustine lets his closest friend die in the full bloom of youth. The conflict comes to a head straight away:

. . . Neither the charm of the countryside nor the sweet scents of a garden could soothe [my soul]. It found no peace in song or laughter, none in the company of friends at table or in the pleasures of love, none even in books or poetry . . . my heart grew sombre with grief, and wherever I looked I saw only death . . . for I was sick and tired of living and yet afraid to die. I suppose that the great love which I had for my friend made me hate and fear death all the more, as though it were the most terrible of enemies, because it had snatched him away from me. I thought that, just as it has seized him, it would seize all others too without warning ... [my soul] only fell and weighed me down once more, so that I was still my own unhappy prisoner, unable to live in such a state and yet powerless to escape from it ... I had become a puzzle to myself ...[2]

Man is in a 'sorry state', compelled to live, and compelled to die; he did not choose to live, he rejects death, and yet death will not pass him by. This is perhaps the first time that anyone has described with such penetration the perfidious cliffs on which all of us run aground at least once in our lives, implicitly at any rate, unless we are the sort of people who are willing to accept a cheap form of happiness based on self-interest; but we know for certain that somewhere within each of us there is a borderline between life and death. We cannot deny an Existential event of this sort out of existence simply by calling it nonsensical or incongruous, and we cannot avoid or escape it either; but then nor can we stand up for it without making some attempt to progress beyond it. Until then there can be no solution to the problem, which can take on a supra-individual importance that is of value to the whole of mankind, but can equally well lead to despair and desolation.

Augustine tells how this feeling of boundlessness that he had experienced when he came face to face with death for the first time gradually evaporated in later life; after all he was only twenty-two when his friend died. Augustine uses the words 'fickleness', 'inconstancy' and 'searching' as the keynote in his description of what happened to him later. He is at pains to make his readers sense the fickleness of all things transient, the frailty of life on the sea of human existence, and how near tears shed at parting are to death. Concrete events, everyday occurrences – death is always near at hand and it can come upon us at any moment. Then he leaves Carthage, runs away from his mother, undertakes a dangerous sea-voyage, has a bad attack of consumption in Rome, is thwarted in his ambitious plans, goes to Milan – St Augustine says that all this indicates that he is really running away from himself and from death, which is at work inside him. Everything becomes relative in his eyes. The problems pile up: the problem of time, the problem of good and evil, the problem of the spirit as compared to the transitory nature of the senses. And reason is silent. As the claims of reason become more and more impossible to fulfil, his scepticism deepens:

I wanted to be just as certain of these things which were hidden from my sight as that seven and three make ten . . .[3]

Augustine reconstructs a monologue spoken by him during this period of his life, showing how his scepticism gradually loses ground in the face of reason and allows his confidence in unreason to grow, strengthening his irrationality:

The Academics! What wonderful men they are! Is it true that we can never know for certain how we ought to manage our lives . . . ? No, not that! We must search all the more carefully and never despair. I can see now that the passages in Scripture which I used to think absurd are not absurd at all . . .[4]

But . . . ! There is a solution here, he cries: Christ, the word made flesh, died as a man and yet overcame death. So such a thing is possible, even though it is totally unacceptable, when looked at rationally. So we won't start asking what, why and how.

His irrational religious experience of belief in Christ allows him to overstep the limits of his consciousness, a feat which he could not have achieved by any other means.

Then comes the final act of the drama – the renunciation of life, the revaluation of all values. The renunciation of the will to live, the will to perform the acts of decision demanded of us every day, the will to act at all, represents the final scene in the renunciation of reason.

This is where St Augustine's theology begins; it is a subjectivistic theology concerned with a purely personal experience of God, which helps men to struggle out of the abyss of their own discontinuous existence. In its extreme form it is a type of spiritualism which is insensitive to everything that happens simply and soullessly outside itself, to all things transient. And in this spiritualistic form St Augustine's theology was always being injected with new life as

Christianity developed, whenever the tendency to rationalize belief began to outweigh other factors in institutionalized piety. Augustine's spiritualism will protest against this tendency, aiming to evoke a belief in God which is completely idiotic.

What else is it but idiotic, this scornful disregard for life, recorded in Augustine's *Soliloquies*?

> What I desire to know is God and my soul. And nothing more? Absolutely nothing.[5]

Christianity is thought of here as a passionate desire for an absolute life.

3

But the reader must not succumb to the power of suggestion in St Augustine's *Confessions*. There is another quite different St Augustine, Bishop Augustine this time, who was the author of a large number of polemical and apologetical works, including an important text called *De civitate dei* (*City of God*), which may well be the most important of all.

In this collection of twenty-two books Augustine set out the politico-theological ideology of the Church which, exactly a hundred years earlier, at the beginning of the Emperor Constantine's reign, had become the official Church of the Roman Empire. This means that Augustine is tackling a completely different problem in this book: the problem of order and of 'anti-order', of authority and obedience, justice and power, war and peace, Church and state, actions belonging to the past and the Last Judgement.

All we need to do here is to make a brief list of the fundamental ideas: God's state is to the worldly state as the light is to the dark. But this antithesis cannot be linked to the contrast between heaven and earth, between the eternal and the temporal. The Kingdom of God is a community made up of the elect in Christ as they live, in the past, the present and the future, among those who form the secular city and who will not be finally separated into the saved and the damned until the Last Judgement. So human society is homogeneous in appearance only; in fact it is really divided in two by the boundary line of sin, which also forms the link between life and death. So the very existence of this society represents a struggle, a war between two basic principles, a war which never ceases, and it is impossible to guarantee a lasting peace. Its enemies are the people who belong to the earthly city, and the Christian is quite justified in fighting them – with weapons if necessary – if he is commanded to do so by an authority granted by God; indeed it is his duty to do so.

The object of this battle is to establish an order based on righteousness, which gives each man what he is due and makes sure that he rises up to God. The Church calls upon Christians to obey this order and support it, so that two things can be guaranteed: firstly, the possessions which are necessary for ordinary mortal existence, and secondly, those possessions which help to bring us nearer to God. Any city which does not have these aims in mind is an unlawful city, one huge gang of thieves (*magnum latrocinium*) and must be destroyed. The efforts made by the Church of Rome to encourage the faithful to support an institution which met them with passive resistance only a short while before reaches its highest point in the political-cum-theological work of St Augustine.

What happened to the apocalyptic Christianity proclaimed by Jesus in the three hundred years after his death? and who exactly was this Augustine?

4

Jesus's radical thinking about decisive actions did not lead the Jews to make a practical protest. They did, it is true, wage war on Rome, but this was a purely local affair and it ended in tragedy for Israel. The Kingdom of God, which Jesus expected them to find 'already on the morrow', seemed to slip further and further away from the early Christians and the first Christian communities, both in time and in space. And as it did so, the human form of their murdered prophet disappeared from their field of vision and soared ever upwards to the firmament on its way to heaven.

What was once an act of choice motivated by love becomes a belief in that love which has departed from us. Love is searched

for incessantly, constant efforts are made to keep in touch wit
God is no longer a direct summons, but the object of a longing
which is constantly rekindled; and of religious deliberations. These
deliberations are particularly affected by a wide variety of late
Hellenistic influences, which include heathen elements from the
classical world as well as Oriental ones.

Christianity did gain a foothold in the Roman world and even
began to spread, although it was constantly being persecuted: it
fascinated people by the depth and determination of its protest and
by its hoministic spirit. But over the first two hundred years it
developed inwardly along the lines of an increasingly vigorous and
irrational attitude about belief, which is intended to shield it from
the dangers of the classical world. As the early Christians struggled
on with such rugged determination they had no idea that they
were in fact obscuring and destroying Jesus's original message and
giving it a false mystical interpretation; that they were falling into
the very trap that they had been trying so energetically to avoid.

We only have to listen to Tertullian (A.D. 150–220), who was one
of the early Fathers:

Wretched Aristotle! who taught them dialectic, that art of building up
and demolishing, so protean in statement, so far-fetched in conjecture,
so unyielding in controversy, so productive of disputes; self-stultifying,
since it is ever handling questions but never settling anything ... What
is there in common between Athens and Jerusalem? What between the
Academy and the Church? What between heretics and Christians? ...
After Jesus Christ we desire no subtle theories, no acute enquiries after
the Gospel.[6]

This rejection of the rational thinking of the Greeks, which represents a conscious rejection of rationality in general, leads the author
to conclude:

The Son of God was born: shameful, therefore there is no shame. The
Son of God died: absurd, and therefore utterly credible. He was buried
and rose again: impossible and therefore a fact ...[7]

The tension which stemmed, along with the message attributed
to Jesus, from the inner struggle for an act of love, an act intended
to burst open the future, now becomes a duel between reason and

emotion; and this duel does not lead to a satisfactory solution. If we accept this view, a miracle can only take place within us, and we will be completely at a loss to understand it; so the more inexplicable it is, the more it deserves our confidence. Not God, but Plotinus's *logos*, whose transformation into flesh was equally inexplicable, is the direct challenge. Everything splits up, disintegrates, dissolves into a dualistic attitude: man is here – God is over there; the body here – the soul there; evil here – good there; the earthly kingdom here – the Kingdom of Heaven there. How do we bridge the unbridgeable?

It seems at first that the only possible solution is the one given by St Augustine in his *Confessions*. But this can only acquire a specific meaning if we think of Christ as an individual, unconnected with his community. But in reality the Christian is always faced with the fact of belonging to the Church, to a community which is firmly entrenched in the world and in time.

As Christianity spread, its adherents were compelled, whether they wanted to or not, to have it out with the political ideology of Rome in the first centuries A.D. and come to some sort of a compromise with it. We must remember that right from the outset the classical conception of the cosmos and its crystal-clear organization seemed peculiar to the people of Israel, with their monistic religion based on choosing and action. They thought of it as 'heathen'. Jesus's message and Christianity as expressed in the Apocalypse, which revived the old dynamism of Israel, opposed the classical spirit, thinking of it now not merely as an unfamiliar doctrine, but as a dangerous enemy who must be challenged in no uncertain terms. But tackling an enemy always involves the tacit admission that this enemy has actually infiltrated our own ranks. The first Christian communities are compelled to seek some sort of compromise with the politics of Rome and their concept of the commonwealth or *polis*. The ancient Greeks' idea of the *polis* was tantamount to 'a common homeland' or 'communal living' (*synoikismos*) in the motionless and timeless space of the cosmos. Its existence was controlled by a law (*nomos*) which was of the mythical-cumcosmic nature; it acted on the commonwealth from outside, as did the *polis* of the gods. Its orientation was thus objective and it was the source on the one hand of polytheism and on the other of technical skill. The practical events which take place in the commonwealth gradually force this orientation to rationalize the mythical law.

Solon, and later Plato and Aristotle, all attempted to do this, but such attempts ended in the crisis of Attic democracy. Under Alexander the Great the concept of the *polis* expanded considerably. It had already changed from being a mythical-cum-cosmic idea to a *cosmopolitan* concept which was thought of in highly concrete terms, both from the military angle and from the political angle: the commonwealth as Alexander wanted it to be understood in his plans for world dominion was to be a sort of centre between the large world of the cosmos, into which man is irrevocably placed, and the small world of human existence. It was to occupy the empty spaces in which man would lose himself if it were not for the intervention of politics.

Alexander fails. And even Greece itself is eventually beaten. The conqueror adopts the ideas of his conquered enemy and alters them to suit his own requirements and under the pressure of circumstances. The Roman Empire sees the whole cosmos as no less than an analogy of the Roman commonwealth. Its laws are the laws of the cosmos, or should be. But *we* find a simile for the laws of the cosmos in the image of the human organism, which functions so harmoniously.

The might of Rome declined in the Hellenistic world, and the idea of the cosmopolis became further and further removed from political reality. And as this happened, the idea turned out to be increasingly absurd and the reality proved to be thoroughly terrestrial.

The yawning gulf of history opens up.

Christianity, which is expanding on the same political and social basis, now develops in the opposite direction: it transcends the narrow boundaries of Israel, gaining ground among the pagans as well as among the Jews and taking root throughout the Roman Empire, though particularly in Rome itself. Consciously or unconsciously, willingly or unwillingly, it becomes cosmopolitan. The fate of Christianity coincides more and more with the future of the

Empire and vice versa. The Christians who lived in the first centuries A.D. still have, somewhere at the very heart of their being, the Israelites' deep understanding of history and of the decisions which must spring from love. But the ensuing act must come to terms with the concrete cosmos of politics and the current political balance of power. The Christian finds himself forced to reflect on the consequences of his actions, and on the responsibility he accepts by acting in such a way. The idea of history as time; the idea of the cosmos as space; the conflict between love and power: that is the Church's problem.

The Edict of Milan (313) created a new situation for the solution of the conflict. Christianity entered the age of Constantine.

This event had certain inescapable consequences; instead of being persecuted, as it had been previously, the Church became the imperial Church of Rome; in 325 the Council of Nicaea formulated a compulsory canon of Triniterian dogma and so constituted its theology *de jure*. And in 413 St Augustine began to write the first of his twenty-two books on the City of God.

5

Now who was St Augustine?

Was he a man who had been utterly shattered by the experience of death, or was he an adherent of *Realpolitik* in the Church of Rome? Did he have a soul which pined for God – or was he an authority among the Fathers who sought a justification for the city/state exercising power, and for acts of military violence? Should we see him as one of the founders of the philosophical study of man; as providing, with his passionate heart and incomparable fervour, an outline of the drama of human existence? Or wasn't he rather the Church's first political ideologist? What exactly is he, among all these alternatives?

Two extreme attitudes meet and indeed clash together with unusual vehemence and abruptness in St Augustine's personality. Both these attitudes belong to post-Constantinian Christianity and each has its own stamp, since they owe their existence to utterly different spiritual and cultural traditions, one classical and the other Jewish.

It is true that their concrete historical form is now substantially different from the original prototype – the static classical concept of space has been replaced by the Hellenistic idea of the cosmopolis; and the dynamic Jewish concept of time as a call for a decision involving a historical act has evolved into a transcendental idea which stakes an absolute claim to belief, so that the shattered individual cannot transcend the horizon of death without the help of belief. There is no way of passing from one attitude to the other: if we give preference to one, we only distort the other; if we emphasize one, the other becomes stunted. A politically ambitious form of Christianity which allies itself with temporal power sins against belief, whether it likes it or not, and causes the faithful to protest. But anyone who seeks refuge in the world of belief and subjective religious transcendence becomes a stranger to the world, and no longer counts in temporal society. That is the dilemma of post-Constantinian Christianity.

St Augustine tried to overcome this dilemma, but in vain. He is shattered by the thought of death because he is a *Realpolitiker*. He is a *Realpolitiker* because he is shattered by the thought of death. He is both of these at the same time: he is a 'sorry state'. He tears apart something which originally formed a single unit: the decision to act which is motivated by passionate love is reduced to a passionate belief in love itself; the Lord as an appeal addressed to the present is transformed into Christ, who has ascended into heaven, into a transcendental god, into a mysterious physical substance. All that is left of the risk entailed in action is the shattering experience of death. The lived and living monistic belief is transformed into a dualistic theology of man and god, body and soul, life and death. The dangerous dynamism of history is exchanged for the re-establishment of order in the cosmos by means of Christianity; of course in both cases man must inevitably die.

Augustine is a *portrait of the Church in time and space*; he is a Father of the Church.

Is there a way out of this dilemma? A solution which could be called Christian? It is not for me to decide. Yet I do feel that there is a way out. That it would consist of reverting anew to the appeal voiced by Jesus and by the Apocalypse. Getting back *anew*: this would mean that both the cosmopolitan orientation of Christianity and the shattering experience of death, that experience which stakes an absolute claim to belief, would have to be *overcome*; it would mean that the decisive passion for an act of love which bursts open the womb of the future and overcomes, if not death, at least the fear of death would have to be restored to the Christian.

Somewhere here, in this once 'sorry state' which is 'sorry' no longer, all of us, atheists and Christians alike, can come together.

Footnotes

1) St Augustine: *Confessions*, translated by R. S. Pine-Coffin, Penguin, 1961. Book III, pp. 58–9.

2) op. cit. Book IV, pp. 78, 76, 77, 78, 76.

3) op. cit. Book VI. p. 116.

4) op. cit. Book VI, p. 126.

5) St Augustine: *Soliloquia animae ad Deum*, I, ii, 7.

6) Tertullian: *De praescriptione haereticorum*, VII, translated by Henry Bettenson in *Documents of the Christian Church*, O.U.P., 1963.

7) Tertullian: *De carne Christi*, 5, translated by Henry Bettenson, in *The Early Christian Fathers: A selection of the writings of the Fathers from St Clement of Rome to St Athanasius*, O.U.P., 1956.

4

ST THOMAS AQUINAS

Intellect and Faith

1

Early in the year 1225 (the most probable date), Thomas, the seventh and youngest of the sons of Landulf, Count of Aquino, and Theodora of Theate (Chieti in the Abruzzi) was born in his father's castle at Roccasecca, not far from Naples. Landulf belonged to the Lombard nobility: his mother, Francesca di Suabia, was the sister of Frederick Barbarossa; Theodora was the descendant of Norman nobles. The complementary talents of North and South, transmitted through a dual lineage of nobility, blended in the child and produced a marvellously well-tempered body, selected to become the instrument of a mind excelling all minds in wisdom, the maker of unity. He came into the world at the beginning of a century when Christian civilization – already imperilled and in imminent danger of dissolution – was on the point of righting itself again to put forth its supreme fruit. Vast conflicts were everywhere waged but dominated in spite of everything by the order of the spirit, war, politics, poetry and religion, the duel between the Pope and the Emperor, the power of feudalism and the power of the Church, the pride of the strong, the virtues of the Saints; he came at the most lustily, most starkly human moment of mediaeval humanity. His mother, who was to stop at nothing to prevent his following the will of God, was a woman of great virtue and self-denial. And while his brothers, rather than see him as a mendicant religious, thought nothing of inciting him to mortal sin, his sister Theodora, Countess of San Severino, was to spend her life in works of mercy and penance and leave behind her a memory of sanctity.

One day, as his nurse was about to give him his bath, the little Tommasso snatched up a piece of parchment, which not for worlds would he leave go, and wept so copiously that he had to be bathed with his fist clenched. His mother came upon the scene and, in spite of his wailing and screaming, forced the hand open; the angelic greeting was written upon the piece of parchment.[1]

Jacques Maritain, a modern Catholic writer, uses great skill in choosing the style of his narrative, which allows us to appreciate the impressive simplicity of the naïve legends attached to the saints. But St Thomas himself is above such legends: anything we know of the life of this learned Schoolman is utterly colourless. The only thing we know for certain is that he read theology at the University of Naples. In the 1340s he entered the Dominican order, in spite of strong opposition from his parents, who shut him up for a considerable length of time. He managed to escape, going first to Naples, then to Paris and finally to Cologne, where he completed his studies under the guidance of Albert the Great. The rest of his life was shared between the University of Paris and Rome, and was filled with theological work and controversy. The books which were the fruit of this productive period 'weighed as much as a horse'; they are pugnacious books and were severely attacked. St Thomas died when he was not quite fifty.

The philosophy and theology which he bequeathed to posterity was accepted as the official doctrine of the Church shortly after his death. It enjoyed years of brilliant prosperity, and then suffered a decline in the eyes of the academic world. Itself a product of the erudition of the Schoolmen, it got caught between the millstones of Scholasticism and was ground down to such a fine powder that it soon became utterly indigestible. It seemed as if it were finished for good.

And yet its influence kept on increasing for several decades, both inside and outside the Roman Catholic Church. It was honoured with the august name of *philosophia perennis*, a philosophy which outlives the centuries and is fit to become a spiritual prop for everything and everybody. Its severely self-contained Gothic system contains more than later philosophies, streaming out in all directions, are willing to admit; but on the other hand, not so much that its structure is not also threatened by the upheavals which take place over the centuries. The Humanists of the nineteenth century thought of St Thomas as belonging entirely to the period 'before the light dawned'; they saw his philosophy as a corpse with rouged cheeks from which the traces of death had been wiped off, so that it looked as if it were alive, although in fact it was already stinking.

The Marxists, too, regarded the figure of Thomas and his work in the same light, in so far as they had not already gone beyond the hostility dictated by the Enlightenment alone. His *Summa* seemed to them ingenious and abstruse. Hundreds of questions, split up into sub-questions, sub-divided in their turn into thousands of sections and sub-sections; a confused and unwieldy system, weighed down with an excessive number of circumlocutions in its terminology and with casuistic pros and cons in its arguments; countless references to the 'Holy Scriptures' and 'other authorities'; a mixture of magical fantasies and absurd fairy-stories. And yet they came across it over and over again in life and in their battles and got to know it as a doctrine which is always changing and therefore remains alive.

How can the spirit of the Middle Ages intervene in the discussions which take place in our own day?

2

The Middle Ages? Anyone who has missed having a general education thinks that this stage of history is represented by a dark chasm, a stagnant, marshy stretch of water with shreds of mist floating above it and lit merely by the faint glow of will-o'-the-wisps flickering amid poisonous sulphur vapours. But looming out of this medieval 'smog' we can see the towers of Romanesque basilicas and the pointed spires of Gothic cathedrals. Isn't that type of architecture dead and gone long ago? Or are the cathedrals perhaps the architectonic idealization of an order which was deliberately hewn out of stone so that it could survive the centuries? Their complicated message can be read with confidence by anyone who does not limit the concept of feudalism to the fundamental social and economic situation; it is precisely this insight into the circumstances which will give him an understanding of the remarkable way medieval theology endeavoured to discover the general standards and architectural laws of a human society capable of enduring for all eternity.

Unlike the Gothic cathedrals, whose sublime beauty continues to amaze us centuries later, the theologian failed to reap success.

Failure was inevitable. Yet this does not detract from the value of his adventurousness or his design. The pattern of the questions posed by Thomas Aquinas can still interest us, although we are not in the least interested in the direction his answers took. But that is enough, if we want to re-examine the stereotyped ideas which people held about him. The main thing to remember is this: the Church was the only institution capable of helping the anonymous men and women of the Middle Ages to obtain insight into the essence and spirit of their general significance as human beings. The term 'Catholic' originally signified 'the universal man'. The concept of universality was naturally more than a mere idea. It was understood in concrete terms, and limited in the institutional sense to a man 'devoted to the Roman form of sacred things'.[2] The gulf between the feudal lord and his bondman could be bridged only on the level of the Church and the Christian religion, and, even then, only where we define things in the most general terms. Neither lord nor bondman confronts the last and deepest religious principles as an individual to whom independence has been granted, but in the first instance in generally human and hoministic terms – as a member of the human race. This supersedes the view of slavery which sees the slave as a mere instrument who happens to be able to speak; and draws a dividing line down the middle of mankind to separate the human world from the non-human world. The Christian knows that he has been allocated a certain fate. *Sumus homines.* But this allocation applies solely on the level of the fundamental facts of his race: i.e. procreation and death. Men enter life as men, not as some sort of instrument. And we die as men. Christian theology voices this idea in its doctrines of the soul, of original sin, the forgiveness of sins and the Last Judgement.

But man's entry into the world was in itself an event full of social significance which marked him for the rest of his life. As a rule if he was born in bondage, he also died in bondage, but the man who first saw the light of day in an aristocratic four-poster bed automatically won certain non-transferable social privileges. The difference lay in something which was invisible to the naked eye: the secret of blood. The secret ability of blood to bind people together and separate them was one of the juridical realities of medieval society. It was rooted in the economic situation of the Middle Ages. For the natural economy, which was divided up into a large number of small units but had not yet been amalgamated into one single market, had so far excluded the possibility of creating universal human bondage from the world in which men worked. In such a situation the producer could not yet make an objective assessment of his own value, or reveal his own interest and his own importance. Man, whether he was a serf or an estate-owner, was merely a supplementary trimming to the land, belonging to it and being 'handed down' along with it. We cannot yet detect any idea of real estate here, but a mysterious, sanctified union, something sacred. Man's destiny is a mystery both to the serf and to his master. If we look at the paintings and drawings of the period, we will see that serfs were portrayed as 'objects': not as the subject of a painting or of a story but as an object belonging to their master, who regards them with benevolence and affection. But by the same token, the serf doesn't think of his master or other overlords as a distinct personality with individual features. He can only conceive of them as the representatives of their allotted functions and titles. The master's colour, his coat-of-arms, the marks of respect which are his due and which determine his social rank: all these are of vital importance to the serf. The ties are more immediate here, single-minded as they are in their brutality and friendliness; an organic connection, loyalty, emotion. That is why there is no political rule here in the modern sense.

In the Middle Ages the life of the people and the life of the state were identical. Man was the actual principle of the state, but it was man as *unfree*. Thus it was the *democracy of unfreedom*, perfected alienation.[3]

Catholicism and its personification, the Church, is a reflection of these circumstances, with the profane element hidden safely in the sacred element. The Christian religion was at that time the only sphere which had the possibility of being understood by all men. The actual benefits, which had not yet become visible, are symbols of disturbing mysteries. The sensually obvious symbols of the blood, which is shed for the redemption of mankind, and the body, which, although slain, was nevertheless resuscitated and ascended into Heaven, give man a vague idea of what he actually is. They were a model for his hoministic decision to take stock of himself. So it was an alienation, though not a forcible one, which was accepted as a mystery connected with the association between man and nature, an internal arrangement by means of which an exhausted life can be renewed, so that it rises again and again from its musty vault, just as Christ did. The world is still sacred. It does certainly have a few fissures in its surface by now, but they are not enough to threaten the whole structure. It still stands firm and can be taken in at a single glance. It is a logical edifice, and at the same time 'beautiful'.

Its master-builder is Thomas Aquinas. He understands what is necessary for his own time.

3

Four hundred years after the fall of the Roman Empire, when the Christian religion entered mankind's field of vision, it left behind it the ruins of the old world through which it had borne the concept of the *civitas humana*. As yet, it had no idea of what lay ahead.

The monks and the churchmen were virtually the only people in those barbaric times who could read and write and who knew a certain amount about how to till the land and about politics. They worked in the seclusion of the monasteries and at the royal courts. They copied old texts and taught noblemen's sons. They brooded on the question of how missionaries should be sent among the barbarians; they concocted amazing and successful subterfuges behind the scenes in the chambers of the lords of the land; they blessed swords. They were not worried by the reproaches which could be made by future generations. Scotland, France, Germany, Auxerre, Cluny, Paris, Chartres, Fulda, St Gall – these were all centres of Christian activity.

Two or three hundred years later the economic and political situation was stabilized to a certain extent and quarrels arose between the two partners who were in power – the Church and the emperor. There was still a long way to go before the throne of St

Peter was shaken to its very foundations; the Church of Rome was in control of an idea which towered miles above the coarse views of the unruly rulers of worldly society. Their banner with its cross blazed over Europe, armed hordes marched off under their flag to spread belief in Christ and to defend it against the non-Christian curs; they were admittedly also attracted by the idea of looting and robbery. The historian will tell of the rivers of blood which flowed during the crusades, of the satanic background to the party quarrels between the Guelphs and the Ghibellines, of regicide, bishops taking mistresses, and torture-chambers in the monasteries. Yet the real truth cannot be pieced together from this type of historical anecdote. If the historian does not dig down any further than this, the whole idea of Christianity – whose range he has not yet properly understood – will remain alien to him.

When Canon Fulbert's myrmidons, in the remote days of the early Middle Ages, seized hold of Abelard in the depths of the night and castrated him by the light of pine torches, they were performing a thoroughly symbolic act: they were driving a rebellious man, who wanted to be a separate individual, *one* man for *one* woman, back into the indistinguishable uniformity on which the medieval order was based, and which caused its downfall.

Deliberately standing out from the ordinary run of people, emerging above the surface of Catholicism, meant that one was attempting to extricate oneself from the collective fate of mankind, turning one's back on it. The quarrel about the 'universals' – did we, as represented by Adam, sin because we bear the common *name* of man, or because we were already included in this category in *real* terms? – was not merely a piece of presumption raised in the debates of the Schoolmen. It was of vital importance for the welfare of medieval society. The quarrel was conducted round the question of whether the authority of the Church – which is alone in knowing what the world needs – will survive, or whether reason, which is still in its early infancy at this point, will gain control of all that side of things, shouting its sovereignty from the rooftops, just like a tyrant who has not reached maturity and who, when it comes down to it, does not know what he wants and so brings about a catastrophe. It is absolutely essential that this world, which has only just escaped dire chaos, should have some sort of order. At this point, Christianity is the only force to have been working for centuries on the prototype for just such an order: the Kingdom of God. What alternative has reason got to offer? We only need to delve into the problems which beset the period to grasp that there was very little evidence available to support the claims of reason. And into this arena, echoing with arguments, stepped St Thomas.

Totally unsuccessfully, to begin with. So far, Scholasticism was far from being properly prepared to support its ambitious solution to current problems. Jesus's 'Kingdom of God', which he proclaimed to be the fruit of a decision, of a radical choice and a free act, had become increasingly remote in time and space and had split up into two parts, the Kingdom of Earth and the Kingdom of Heaven, this world and the next. Jesus Christ personified the connecting link between these two kingdoms and man's longing to leave his divided state and become a single unit again. Any theology which made its appearance at this moment in time could not but try out methods of achieving this, to see if they were practicable. The Fathers in the first centuries of Christianity's existence, who still had to be on their guard against the pagans of the classical world and were also a prey to the influences of Hellenism, could see only one possibility: belief, belief regardless of all the objections and considerations put forward by reason . . . we can just discern here, as if it came from a very long way off, a last dying echo of the great spirit of Israel. This also applies to St Augustine. In his case there is the additional necessity of consolidating the Church, the mechanism for granting salvation, in this world and the next; he declares, 'I would not even believe the Gospel, if the authority of the Catholic Church did not urge me to do so.'

Later on, the initial opposition to classical culture, which had been fed by propaganda, died down, and in these relatively peaceful times the theologians had the time to study those works which were the product of reason and classical culture. So they turned straight away to Boethius, the 'last of the Romans', then from him via Plotinus back to Plato and Aristotle, and began to examine their initially negative attitude. The tranquil periods of reflection in the monasteries also bore fruit. The churchmen sensed that in the complicated situation in which the world now found itself, when it was only just beginning, very slowly, to see clearly, the simple faith of the Fathers was no longer enough; although it is still essential as a basis for the order which must be established. St Anselm of Canterbury (eleventh century) knew that the Catholic (i.e. universal) belief in the Kingdom of God was the starting-point for each and every productive piece of reasoning, and represented the spiritual sphere into which every item can be integrated and connected with everything else. If we understand the connection between reason and belief in this light, it has very little in common with the relationship which the later individualist and rationalist eras reacted to in such a touchy and irritated manner. At this point it would never have occurred to anyone that reason could break down, when belief held sway and the conflict was hopeless. The ecclesiastical theologian who lived in the Christian Middle Ages was socially committed as an individual; he saw the Church as a force capable of fashioning the world of man in universal terms; of using its powers of organization to put its stamp on a society which is still afflicted by the consequences of the various shocks it has sustained, and is held together only by a great effort. He saw the Church as possessing that spiritual strength which 'knows' – through belief – and feels called upon to accept responsibility. It is true that his practical influence is accompanied by interests and activities which have nothing to do with his mission except in name, as is always the case when any restricted community commits itself to action. But this should not mislead us into painting a false picture of the whole problem. If we do not wish to project later problems into this period, we must not be satisfied with assessing them in a purely ironic manner and talking about the Middle Ages having subjugated reason to belief and seen philosophy as the handmaiden of theology. In those days this was a highly progressive process, however incredible it may sound to a rationalist critic. But St Thomas was both the culmination of this process and its outermost limit.

Unlike his theological contemporaries of the Augustinian and Franciscan schools, who vacillated between a highly incomplete knowledge of Plato and Aristotle on the one hand and the Gospels on the other, St Thomas is the first real Aristotelian in the Christian Church. Unlike those who sought either a purely rational way out of the impasse of the Schoolmen's philosophy, or alternatively a purely mystical one – which in the circumstances could be no more than a cutting through an impenetrable thicket of connections, of which no one could say where it would lead – Thomas is a thinker and theologian who knows what reason is capable of, and what it has to accomplish within the framework of religious doctrines. The relationship between reason and belief is clearly defined: he calls for a belief which is capable of achieving so much intellectually that it can penetrate the order of reality and derive from it a compulsory prototype for this order.

In Aristotle he encounters the first philosopher to see that the cosmic order is arranged horizontally, to find its causal links, its boundaries and its passageways, to point out that everything in the cosmos is harmoniously balanced, from pure matter, which represents a mere possibility, to pure form, which is full reality. Thomas's study of Aristotle, whose work had now been translated virtually in its entirety, led him to the conclusion that the essence of his philosophy was a unique cosmo*logical* idea; an idea capable of occupying and dividing up that anxiety-inducing space of history which the Christian faith grapples with in an inner struggle, collapsing secretly under the weight of it.

St Thomas is thrilled by Aristotle. At the same time he does undoubtedly sense that he lacks something which medieval man obtained through faith and the theologian through theology; what he lacks is the sense of being hurled into time, the curse which hangs over all things temporal, the dissonance which man bears within him in spite of everything and which had no place in Aristotle's efforts to make things harmonious. Thomism is one of the first serious attempts to connect and reconcile the two basic dimensions of man – the cosmic dimension and the historical dimension, and to use them to create a prototype for an order which could be seen as a definitive solution. This attempt was not fated to succeed.

Aristotle is not in a position to fill the whole realm of belief. He may be able to help us to articulate space by means of structures arranged in hierarchies, running upwards from the earth to the

Thrones of the Heavens. But for the believer there is always a place left over in which he stands alone once again at his allotted post in this excessively rigid order, shouting out his loneliness into the cosmos. Then the whole elaborate structure falls in like a house of cards and all the rational evidence that suggests it is a permanent fixture becomes meaningless. Man turns back inside himself, to the most unfathomable places of all, and finds nothing but himself, abandoned, wretched – and completely devoid of belief.

Thomism knows this; that is why it relies so heavily on the external power of an unchangeable hierarchy. The Thomists want to construct a socio-political structure which will survive the ages, although it can always only be valid for one given period. Since it was totally keyed to objective order and to penetrating this order by means of the intellect, Thomism eventually lost its subtle flair for knowing man's real inner needs. It wanted to reilluminate the soul which is asking questions or feels forsaken and sunk in despair, by offering words of consolation which at best appeal to our sense of architectonic skill. As if proof could satisfy those whose belief has dwindled away, in whom hope and love have faded, that God is outside, remote, as concrete as a stone, as tangible as the night!

After all, if we dig right down to the roots of Christian belief, it is initially far more an act of choosing and deciding, here and now, a decision in which man's whole being actively bursts open the womb of tomorrow and new space. At this moment, the antagonism between what is rational and logical and what cannot be comprehended by the reason is only very slight: it is a moment of practical dynamism. The mind is not lost in space, the reason does not cry out in vain. What is missing in Thomism is the quality of open-mindedness. It will always be an obstacle to the type of belief which has a living sense of man's destiny.

4

Looking at St Thomas Aquinas in this light does not by any means involve relegating him to a position somewhere on the fringes of the history of human thought and intellectual life. The Marxist does not think of Marx's philosophical materialism as an end in itself; still less does he think of it as a supreme arbitrator which measures the historical achievements of the spirit by itself alone. Marxist materialism is interested in establishing the historical justification of every single stage reached in the course of its development, and also of course in establishing where this justification ends. It makes a searching investigation of everything which attempted, in conditions which were historically inevitable, to establish an order which would give a firm basis to man's existence on earth. In other words, it asserts – and it appears to have good reason for doing so – that in every attempt of this kind we can discover something which is worthy of our notice, something which should not be overlooked or forgotten.

On the threshold of a new age, when the old orders crumble away and new ones have not yet evolved, it is obviously very important to think in terms of thousands of years at a time. It seems to me that this is by no means an exorbitant requirement in the case of Communism.

St Thomas was concerned with this question in his own time. This should be enough to make him an enthralling figure for us. Of course he did not ask all the questions which we want answered. And yet – it sometimes seems as if they were all twinkling away in the play of colours in the refracted light at the edges of this excessively rational system, which is articulated into hundreds of questions, thousands of sub-questions, into the 'pros' and the 'cons'.

We reject Thomism because it contains a cosmic and theistic concept of order. But we are in favour of its being studied in a responsible manner – precisely because of this concept. This is our 'pro' and our 'con'.

Footnotes

1) Jacques Maritain: *St Thomas Aquinas, the Angel of the Schools*, translated by J. F. Scanlan, Sheed & Ward, 1931, p. 77.

2) The official Latin formula runs *Homo catholicus – romanae sacrorum formulae addictus.*

3) Karl Marx: *Critique of Hegel's Philosophy of the State*, in *Writings of the Young Marx on Philosophy and Society*, edited and translated by Lloyd D. Easton and Kurt H. Guddell, Anchor, 1967.

5

PASCAL

The 'Infinite' in Mathematics and in Man

1

One of the things schoolboys learn when they enter the mysterious world of physics and nature is the theorem: 'Pressure applied anywhere to an enclosed body of fluid is transmitted equally in all directions.' It is Pascal's Law of Pressure.

Later on, when they study descriptive geometry, they adopt Pascal's views on hexagons and straight lines. The great mathematician and physicist formulated them at the age of sixteen.

Later still, they will come across him again when they study the theory of probabilities and the infinitesimal calculus. This will give them some idea of what chance and infinity are all about.

Engrossed in the secrets of nature and passionately eager to get nature's system – a system composed of objects – under control, they create the artificial world of technology. Most probably they will never learn that Pascal also wrote the following:

This is where unaided knowledge brings us. If it is not true, there is no truth in man, and if it is true, he has good cause to feel humiliated; in either case he is obliged to humble himself . . .

Let man then contemplate the whole of nature in her full and lofty majesty, let him turn his gaze away from the lowly objects around him; let him behold the dazzling light set like an eternal lamp to light up the universe, let him see the earth as a mere speck compared to the vast orbit described by this star, and let him marvel at finding this vast orbit itself to be no more than the tiniest point compared to that described by the stars revolving in the firmament. But if our eyes stop there, let our imagination proceed further . . . The whole visible world is only an imperceptible dot in nature's ample bosom. No idea comes near it; it is no good inflating our conceptions beyond imaginable space, we only bring forth atoms compared to the reality of things. Nature is an infinite sphere whose centre is everywhere and circumference nowhere ...

Let man, returning to himself, consider what he is in comparison with what exists; let him regard himself as lost, and from this little dungeon, in which he finds himself lodged, I mean the universe, let him learn to take the earth, its realms, its cities, its houses and himself at their proper value.

What is a man in the infinite?

But, to offer him another prodigy equally astounding, let him look into the tiniest things he knows. Let a mite show him in its minute body incomparably more minute parts, legs with joints, veins in its legs, blood in the veins, humours in the blood, drops in the humours, vapours in the drops: let him divide these things still further until he has exhausted his powers of imagination, and let the last thing he comes down to now be the subject of our discourse. He will perhaps think that this is the ultimate of minuteness in nature.

I want to show him a new abyss. I want to depict to him not only the visible universe, but all the conceivable immensity of nature enclosed in this miniature atom. Let him see there an infinity of universes, each with its firmament, its planets, its earth ... and finding the same thing yet again in the others without end or respite, he will be lost in such wonders, as astounding in their minuteness as the others in their amplitude. For who will not marvel that our body, a moment ago imperceptible in a universe, itself imperceptible in the bosom of the whole, should now be a colossus, a world, or rather a whole, compared to the nothingness beyond our reach? Anyone who considers himself in this way will be terrified at himself, and, seeing his mass, as given him by nature, supporting him between these two abysses of infinity and nothingness, will tremble at these marvels. I believe that with his curiosity changing into wonder he will be more disposed to contemplate them in silence than investigate them with presumption.

For, after all, what is man in nature? A nothing compared to the infinite, a whole compared to the nothing, a middle point between all and nothing, infinitely remote from an understanding of the extremes; the end of things and their principles are unattainably hidden from him in impenetrable secrecy.

Equally incapable of seeing the nothingness from which he emerges and the infinity in which he is engulfed.

What else can he do, then, but perceive some semblance of the middle of things, eternally hopeless ... Who can follow these astonishing processes? The author of these wonders understands them: no one else can.[1]

2

Now, is Pascal a brilliant scientist?

Or is he merely a philosopher without any systematic training behind him who has grasped the importance of scepticism, but rejects it?

Or is he a highly-strung theologian pursuing his hopeless meditations right to the very brink of Church orthodoxy?

It is perfectly obvious that he is all these rolled into one. At the same time, over and above this, he is a man who spent his short and passionate life wracked by physical sufferings which never gave him a moment's respite, the result of an illness from which he was released by an untimely death. The experiment which was his consuming passion was aimed at making God fill the chasm in nature he had known and experienced.

As far as the rationalist critic of religion is concerned, that is all there is to Pascal. He will classify the paradox of a scientist being deeply religious as one of those unfathomable perversities of human nature.

But when a Marxist comes to deal with Pascal, he will be led to ask questions which go far beyond the interpretations given by those who see him as one of the forerunners of Existentialism. He will find himself face to face with a representative of the Pleiad who founded modern science, a man who has passed beyond their purely objective questions and has begun to inquire into the meaning of man's eagerness to find things out.

The modern reader may possibly pull up here in amazement: is it really possible that people ask this sort of question? Can anyone feel any doubt about a goal which involves gaining control of nature, becoming the Lord of Nature, a goal which represents the very core of all scientific research? Isn't this ambition to govern nature one of man's natural characteristics? And if we question it are we not in fact threatening man's very existence? Or perhaps even in this field, where man longs to make his presence felt, there are certain limits which may not be overstepped?

This type of question leads us in two different directions. Firstly, we will be anxious to find out what Pascal the scientist thinks of God. Secondly, our interest in Pascal will gradually be transformed into an interest in one extreme case in the whole Odyssey of classical science, the case of an exceptionally acute mind broaching problems which are normally never given an airing.

3

But we must first listen to a brief account of Pascal's life, though this cannot be absolutely definitive in all details, because even his early biographers tended to use their account to ward off some of his opponents.

But later research, too, although it holds aloof from party squabbles, does not shed any very clear light on his highly passionate personality. Some authors paint a portrait of an unfathomably demonic being who tortured others as violently as himself and attracted attention by his unquestionable genius, but at the same time repelled people by his implacable hatred for everything which provoked his opposition; they portray him as a brutal and explosive character.

Others found in him an early version of those struggles which Kierkegaard was later to fight with such vehemence, which shattered Nietzsche and made Dostoyevsky's Ivan Karamazov suffer so terribly. They find themselves remembering the Existentialist drama undergone by St Augustine, although Pascal's state of mind was in fact quite different.

There are yet others who see him as an impassioned Christian fanatic, a fiery heart which from the moment of its final conversion is interested in nothing but Christ and the absolute. The official Catholic Church reserves its judgement – after all, he was not always orthodox in his belief. But the Protestants, in their turn, found him too Catholic.

Marxist readers will hardly be prepared to put up with the story of his life being reduced to any one moment of his existence. The overall portrait of a man who does not hold himself aloof, but takes an active part in everything which his own era has to offer, will always reflect – in a unique metamorphosis – the whole range of contemporary social circumstances; these are of course quite different in scale from the experiences undergone by the individual in his short life-span, and from the areas where he can exert his influence. So the reader who looks at it this way will think of Pascal's life as a crystal mirroring the historical world around him in its polished facets and surfaces, *creating a replica which is seen in this way and in no other.*

This means that we simply cannot overlook – or pass over with a few brief comments – the fact that right from his childhood, during which he gave such clear proof of his aptitude for mathematics, Pascal never abandoned his scientific life at any point. In his father's home he came under the influence of the great mathematicians of the period, Fermat, Mersenne, Roberval, and this influence increased when he began to work on his own. He began to enlarge the scope of his contacts, both personal contacts and by correspondence, to men such as Desargues, Huyghens, Descartes; when he is enthusiastic about the scientific findings of these gentlemen and also when he disagrees with them, he always shows a lively appreciation of scientific achievement and a systematic interest in scientific methodology, endeavouring to find a precise line of reasoning which should rightly be labelled 'scientific exactitude'. From his early work on the theory of conic sections down to his treatise on roulette (1658), we can detect a clear scientific orientation in his work, and this always permits a resurgence of hope, even in the midst of the profoundest doubts, that he may yet manage to bridge the gulf of emptiness or *vanité*.

Although Pascal's life did sink into just such pits of despair under the repeated attacks of illness, which gave him no respite from the age of twenty-four onwards, it never stopped being the life of a mathematician, physicist and technician, a man who was always enterprising and go-ahead, both in theory and in practice. We only have to think of his design for a calculating machine, which he followed right through to the stage where it was actually constructed, or of his suggestion for a public transport system in Paris in the age of Mazarin – he even made a close study of the economic aspect. Pascal's life cannot be fully understood unless we take these facts into account; Pascal himself cannot be fully understood either – profound Christian that he is: yes, this aspect of him is especially difficult to understand. On the other hand, we must not neglect his social ambitions; these were especially strong during one particular phase of his life, and it is no accident that his sister, Madame Perier, steers tactfully clear of this point in her biography of him. On his arrival in Paris, preceded by a brilliant reputation, all the leading salons in the land opened their doors to him. The fashionable free-thinking ladies and gentlemen who collected at the Marquise de Sablé's and at Madame de Saintot's were a great temptation to an ambitious young man with a middle-class background like Pascal. He was charmed by the Sieur de Méré, by Monsieur de Barreaux, Monsieur Mitton, and especially by the young Duc de Roannez and his sister – he embarked on a lengthy correspondence with her. When he was staying in his summer house he produced a witty and gallant essay on passionate love which was clearly written for her, but was also full of deep devotion and gaiety. He thought of marrying her, for he believed in the strength of their love and felt that such a marriage would help him up the social ladder.

We will probably never know what went wrong. But it seems that Pascal's social ambitions came to an end fairly suddenly and that the collapse of his leanings in this direction hit him as hard as if he had fallen from a great height. Evidence of this can be seen in the annihilating disgust from which Pascal suffered ever after, and his violent loathing of anything which was even remotely connected with the vanity of the life led by smart society.

But this phase of his life did all the same bring him something of considerable value, a feeling for elegance and finesse, for what he was later to call being an *honnête homme*. He had already left far behind him the brutal and primitive fanaticism of the young pro-vincial, a fanaticism which had driven him to violent denunciations even before he left Rouen.

Be that as it may: the loss of his social aspirations compelled Pascal to give another direction to his passionate fervour. The im-petus came from a dramatic incident which took place in Neuilly at the beginning of November 1654, when he slipped under the hoofs of a shying horse and very nearly lost his life. In the full flush of the emotional turmoil this caused he wrote down a few sentences on a scrap of parchment, highly agitated sentences in which the crisis of the last few months came to a head, and which are a sign that his turbulent inner life had taken on a new direction; it is now directed to loving Jesus Christ.

This act of conversion does not mean, however, that Pascal was turning towards a conventional faith. As with everything else he went in for, there was an element of *antagonism* in his new religious attitude, which turned out to be a long-term one; his faith consisted of a continuous series of arguments. Pascal was one of the most zealous adherents of Jansenism, and he played a prominent part in the first wave of a fierce political-cum-religious conflict.

The doctrine of the Dutch bishop Cornelius Jansen (1585–1638) was an independent and moderate version of a predominantly Calvinistic Protestantism within the Catholic Church. Its ideals were the antithesis of the official Thomist doctrine formulated by the Schoolmen, and derived support from St Augustine in stressing the importance of God's grace, which is meted out to men according to his hidden decree. It is true that in this it did quite clearly undermine the authority of the Church as an institute for salvation. But the Church and its leading representatives were totally unwilling to tolerate the disintegration of their attempt to stage a Counter-Reformation.

Pascal's family had been in contact with the Jansenists as early as about 1645. Pascal found their moral and religious truthfulness particularly attractive. Their reciprocal ties were strengthened at the beginning of the 1650s, when Pascal's sister Jacqueline entered the convent of Port-Royal, which was at the very heart of the Jansenist movement. This was also the period of the most violent public quarrels over the teaching of Jansen and Arnauld, which was judged by the Sorbonne in Paris under pressure from the Pope and the King. A combination of various different factors led Pascal to intervene personally in the dispute, and he did so with great energy and vigour. He yearned for radical action which would have an absolute value; and in his defence of this subjective doctrine and its unfathomable religious experience he found something to which he could devote all the unquenched energy of his soul, but he also encountered enemies as determined as himself: these enemies were the Jesuits.

The clash which used up what remained of Pascal's vitality could never have turned out well. In the last months of his life he fell silent, totally absorbed in himself; he died, reconciled with the Church, in 1662, at the age of thirty-nine.

His was a wretched life which ended wretchedly; short and feverish, it was filled with conflicts, both internal and external. The relativity which he came to recognize in nature as well as in society arouses in him over and over again a feeling of horror at the idea of nothingness and a longing for the absolute. He is familiar with the cosmos and the way it swallows man up. He senses that there is an 'infinity' by means of which man can transcend the cosmos.

Pascal sees this boundary between the 'infinite' in mathematics and the 'infinite' in man as the axis on which the Christian faith revolves.

4

Let us now return to our original question: What does God mean to Pascal?

We will be able to give a truthful answer when we know what science meant to him. Pascal is not one of those classical scientists – actually there are very few of them anyway – who are totally absorbed in the business of trying to reach an objective understanding of nature and are completely satisfied with this. An attitude which applies exclusively to objects is always accompanied by reflection aimed at making the most practicable paths to knowledge seem credible, at testing criteria for judging the accuracy of the procedure and the results obtained, and at protesting against any obstacles born of prejudice. Along with most of his contemporaries, Pascal was carried away by the unique possibilities offered by mathematics, especially geometry. Being a geometrician, possessing the 'spirit of geometry' (esprit de géométrie) symbolizes for Pascal the analytical faculty of the mind and is at the same time a proviso that new knowledge can be acquired, i.e. knowledge of a kind hitherto unknown which cannot be deduced from some authority or other. The spirit of geometry is based on a few first principles which are so clear that they do not even need to be proved; it is therefore completely autonomous and free within its own sphere.

Pascal does admittedly know – and in this he sets himself well and truly apart from the other scientists and thinkers of his age – that the possibilities inherent in the spirit of geometry are not to be taken absolutely: he does not prove everything; but anything which is proved is proved without a shadow of doubt. The sublime nature of this way of thinking lies chiefly in the fact that it leads man to an understanding of the infinitely great and the infinitely small: whatever movement, number, dimension or time we think of, it will always be possible to imagine a movement, number etc. which is even larger or even smaller, so that they actually always lie somewhere between nothingness and infinity, but infinitely far away from both.

This thought is still totally geared to the objective approach of the *esprit de géométrie*; it ends with the observation that human beings occupy a position between nothingness and infinity, from the point of view of spatial dimension, number, motion and time. There is, however, no resting-place for man, since there are no limits to define his position, whichever way he looks.

At this point, however, Pascal is already going beyond an objective scientific attitude. As soon as man recognizes that anything which applies to the world of objects is also wholly applicable to himself, any objective consideration, any objective research becomes senseless; it will remain so as long as it is not clear what such a thoroughly relative position means for man himself, or, at bottom, *who man really is*, if he is so irrevocably at the mercy of the extremes of nothingness and infinity.

The objectively analytical spirit of geometry is here confronted by the limits of subjectivism; it goes beyond itself, but falls silent.

The novelty of Pascal's work as a scientist lies in his having the courage to transcend this boundary, and ask himself the radical question of what man as a subjective being signifies. But he goes astray in the territory which he now enters.

How can we get a grip on this territory? Pascal knows that from the point of view of quality this problem is quite different from the one which faces the land surveyor. He now creates the concept of the *esprit de finesse* or 'spirit of refinement'. Unlike the geometrical spirit, which is analytical, taking a few basic axioms as its starting-point, and precision and clarity as its yardstick, *finesse* is a sort of résumé of a whole host of highly sensitive faculties, each one subtly different from the others, which cannot be approached by geometry because it is not sufficiently flexible. They do exist, and they enable us to have a quick glimpse of the situation and to acquire a subtle understanding of it.

Admittedly Pascal is also aware of the danger of subjectivism; he realizes that the *esprit de finesse* is just as one-sided as the *esprit de géométrie*. The thing which precludes one-sidedness, which, as Pascal sees it, creates a balance between the objective process and the subjective process, is the heart, *le cœur*. By this he means not just pure sentiment or emotion, but that inner tension which draws the contrasting elements together into a single unit, creating a constant coherence within man: a powerful and dramatic idea that man, although only a reed, is nevertheless greater than the whole of the universe.

So Pascal continues to set great store by science. It remains indispensable, for without it man cannot become aware of his true position. But science as a practical and spiritual outlook is inadequate: it lets man down at the moment when it has abandoned him to the icy gales of the cosmos. It is weak on the human side, since it falls silent where man begins to ask questions.

But what exactly is Pascal's subjectivism?

First of all he examines the atheistic scheme which it involves:

I do not know who put me into the world, nor what the world is, nor what I am myself. I am terribly ignorant about everything. I do not know what my body is, or my senses, or my soul, or even that part of me which thinks what I am saying, which reflects about everything and about itself, and does not know itself any better than it knows anything else.

I see the terrifying spaces of the universe hemming me in, and I find myself attached to one corner of this vast expanse without knowing why I have been put in this place rather than that, or why the brief span of life allotted to me should be assigned to one moment rather than another of all the eternity which went before me and all that which will come after me. I see only infinity on every side, hemming me in like an atom or like the shadow of a fleeting instant. All I know is that I must soon die, but what I know least about is this very death which I cannot evade.

Just as I do not know whence I come, so I do not know whither I am going. All I know is that when I leave this world I shall fall for ever into nothingness or into the hands of a wrathful God, but I do not know which of these two states is to be my eternal lot. Such is my state, full of weakness and uncertainty. And my conclusion from all this is that I must pass my days without a thought of seeking what is to happen to me. Perhaps I might find some enlightenment in my doubts, but I do not want to take the trouble, nor take a step to look for it: and afterwards, as I sneer at those who are striving to this end (whatever certainty they have should arouse despair rather than vanity), I will go without fear or foresight to face so momentous an event, and allow myself to be carried off limply to my death, uncertain of my future state for all eternity.[2]

So Pascal acknowledges that atheism is really a subjective theory. But it is a totally inadequate theory as far as he is concerned: partly because it pays too great a tribute to the objective attitude of science, going no further than a mere denial; and partly because science, having got rid of God (either altogether or in the form of a compromise), leaves man literally nothing which might give him the opportunity of becoming his own master. The principle of God is for Pascal a positive human principle of nature, which gives man the very first opportunity of making himself felt as a subjective being and developing this aspect of himself; this means that he will not only take possession of nature from the technical point of view, but will do so as a man, or in other words as a being which transcends nature. On the other hand, Pascal sees atheism as saddled with the cowardly attempt to sidestep the most crucial questions. But in so doing it endangers certain basic human values. This signifies to Pascal a life which is not up to the standard of humanity.

He sees theism as the only practicable approach.

But he cannot accept official Christianity and its Thomist/Scholastic interpretation. Both of them seem to him to be as relative as everything else. The Renaissance and classical science, the

Reformation and the fight against the constraints of Catholic orthodoxy have done their bit. Pascal does stay within the bounds of the Catholic Church, it is true, but his conception of the Christian God can never again be the conventional one, since this has no place for the subjective element.

It is to this subjectivism that he devotes the greater part of his reflections. They form the most powerful passages in his *Pensées*.

The effect is sombre and distressing: man is a creature suspended between the twin abysses of the infinitely small and the infinitely great. He reaches infinitely far beyond nothingness, but is himself swallowed up by infinity. Compared to the cosmos he is a miserable speck of dust, and yet he is greater than the cosmos because he *knows* that he is nothing. His interests, his misery, his boredom, his delights, pleasure and exertions – none of these is lasting. Everything ends in disappointment. His history is a history of uselessness and frustrated hopes. From the moment when he takes his first breath, his life is condemned to end in death.

Imagine a number of men in chains, all under sentence of death, some of whom are each day butchered in the sight of the others; those remaining see their own condition in that of their fellows, and looking at each other with grief and despair await their turn. This is an image of the human condition.[3]

Yet we must not be over-hasty in our judgement of Pascal. He is not trying to use this highly gloomy picture to preach a doctrine which sees the whole universe as totally engulfed in pessimism; he wants it to provoke men into protesting, to challenge them not to put up with such a condition, but to search instead for alternatives. His vision expresses the scientist's conviction that science, if left to its own resources, finishes up in despair and that it can be optimistic only if it is blind. This is the starting-point for Pascal's Christian concept of subjectivism, which is outlined in one of the fragments in the *Pensées* in the following terms.

The Stoics say: 'Withdraw into yourself, that is where you will find peace.' And that is not true.

Others say: 'Go outside: look for happiness in some diversion.' And that is not true: we may fall sick.

Happiness is neither outside nor inside us: it is in God, both outside and inside us.[4]

Pascal asserts that both relationships, the external one – which is focused outwards on to the world of objects – and the internal one – which is directed inwards to the individual subjective being – if taken independently, alienate man from himself. He seeks a dialectical link connecting the two and finds one – where else! – in belief in God.

As far as he is concerned, God, as understood by the Schoolmen and St Thomas Aquinas, is inadequate, for he is a God outside man, in heaven, a God treated as an object by the mind seeking confirmation, a God who can be ontologically proved. A God who is only to be found in Heaven is not God, as far as Pascal is concerned. But nor can he make anything of a God who is merely a lasting and subjective experience, 'my very own private God'.

He thinks of God as a God hidden within man, the Jesus of the Gospels and the divine figures who preceded him: the God of Abraham, Isaac and Jacob. For Pascal, an Existential solution to the problem of subjectivism can be found in such a God, but it is a problem of which he can know nothing. Jesus is the man hidden in God. Jesus is God, confronting us as a man: a God who is both close to us and far away.

Pascal knows perfectly well how shaky this type of belief is. It has nothing to do with rational evidence; emotional evidence cannot convince the unbeliever and is non-transferable. So what can he argue with? What can he use to win others over? Pascal chooses an Existential method: if we place a bet on God, we may lose nothing, but we may equally well win everything. He thinks that the 'wager argument' is so convincing! And yet all that comes out of it is the most pathetic argument ever put forward by a narrow-minded religious hack.

Pascal has relatively little feeling for speculative theology. His belief in Christ relies on his historical existence and therefore on the Gospels being absolutely true word for word. So he sees Christ as a totally personal, substantial mystery, the mystery of man in general, a synonym for subjectivism. Belief in Christ is for Pascal the saving element in his conviction that man can penetrate his own mystery, and can only grasp the meaning of his actions when he finds the link joining his passionate heart to frigid unfeeling nature, in whose infinite space he hangs suspended. It is a belief that all man's work will not fall into a bottomless chasm, but will fill up this chasm.

5

Is Pascal correct in his verdict on classical science? If we say 'yes', we are conceding that he overcomes it intellectually.

But when he transcends the boundary of science he is making a theistic step, a step with the stamp of Christianity; an unorthodox version of Christianity, certainly, but the sort of Christianity which has had its chains so effectively broken by classical science and the philosophy bound up with it.

But this is where the first doubt creeps in: have they really broken its chains? Haven't they in fact simply awakened the idea of freedom? An idea which is certainly very effective in practical terms, because it controls the forces of nature; but all the same it is no more than an idea, the heart of which will not be revealed until much later.

Doubts of this type disrupt the self-confidence of those Marxists who have been trained in traditional Marxism. Up to now they had thought of Renaissance science, which led to such brilliant achievements in the seventeenth century, as an unquestionable and *unequivocal* step forward. As far as they were concerned, it effectively represented the end of the Middle Ages. Ever since then, reason has functioned freely, trampling prejudice into the dust. This was where the foundations were laid for a new image of the universe: this was also where the early stages were worked out of the precision techniques without which the modern world of technology and large-scale industries is inconceivable. Up to now, they considered that they were primarily rooted in the Renaissance, with their attitude to the world and to action which has some meaning, their common sense à la Galileo and their rational, scientifically minded convictions. So far they were convinced that the discovery of a cause or a law of nature would bring in millions and that Michelangelo and Leonardo da Vinci were shining and unsurpassed examples to art throughout the centuries; that the true face of man appeared for the first time in the full flush of youth in the work of Pico della Mirandola; and that the spirit of humanism they professed can be found equally in the greedy, ridiculous, extravagant and colossal figures of Gargantua and Pantagruel and in the robust, tragic, subtle, clownlike, but eternally wise figures in Shakespeare . . .

But now – what can the despairing Christian visionary who is Pascal do about this?

Nothing; except to question everything that is taken as a matter of course.

For: *what* exactly did the Renaissance and the science, art and philosophy of the Renaissance overcome? And *how* did it manage to do so?

Whichever textbook we pick up, we will invariably find an explanation of why the feudal order of the Middle Ages broke down, and an analysis of the economic and social factors which brought about its disintegration. It also seems clear that, beginning with Copernicus, via Galileo, Bruno and Bacon and ending with Newton, the Scholastic spirit of the Middle Ages was finally crushed in all its various manifestations, and that since then it has been vegetating miserably somewhere on the periphery of philosophy, while scientific reasoning is fruitfully engaged in building factories instead of cathedrals.

But this is where we must once again ask the question – and indeed it is in the interest of the factories that we should do so: does this breath-taking new scientific and philosophical attitude *really* go further than the feudal way of thinking current in the Middle Ages? or does it fight its battles solely *within the framework of medieval thought*, thus winning only a partial victory over its opponents? How does the new scientific attitude come to be so fundamentally at variance with the medieval Christian and Thomist attitude?

St Thomas had conceived of a Christian version of Aristotelianism as an order which embraces the whole universe and is constructed on a hierarchical formula, so that it is built vertically upwards from the lowest step to the topmost one. A static, self-contained design, based on the view of the cosmos held by classical antiquity.

The Renaissance and the Renaissance spirit destroys this rigid structure by first of all destroying its supporting arches – the authorities. It manages to do so because it is already convinced that its reason, free of all dogma, is capable of gaining control of things without the help of religion. This sudden acquisition of the object world shows us *at first glance* an image of the world which is diametrically opposed to the order that Aristotelian/Thomist philosophy thought it had discovered. So it is not surprising that reason begins to look like the antithesis of belief, and that, by exploiting all the tactical dodges which must exist in a theocratic society, it enforces independence and autonomy. But is the gap between the self-confidence of reason, which is particularly visible in classical science, and the faith of the Middle Ages really so unbridgeable? Is the new universe revealed to us by Galileo so utterly different from Ptolemy's? If we merely make a superficial comparison, then the answer is certainly 'yes'. But if we go into it more thoroughly, we will begin to see that *this* difference is not as fundamental as all that.

We must bear in mind that Platonic academies sprang up in the Italian Renaissance centres as schools of philosophy teaching the new spiritual outlook; the most famous one was run by Marsilio Ficino (1433–99). New philosophical trends always make their first impact in the form of criticism of the premises underlying the recognized views of current society, and then continue by recreating traditional thinking, so that people suddenly realize all over again how topical and exciting it is.

But what can Renaissance man, thirsting for knowledge and power, find to fascinate him in Plato? After all, the opposition to the 'converted philosopher of Stagira' is not the only decisive factor here, nor, on the other hand, is the idea that Aristotle's opinion is more important in deciding how many teeth a horse has got than actually looking in the wretched animal's mouth. That alone would not be enough to speak for Plato.

As far as these philosophers were concerned, the interest of Plato stemmed from two of his ideas, both of which are an essential part of the spiritual atmosphere of the Renaissance and the sphere in which classical science originated.

The first of these ideas concerns the possibility of personal advancement, with man progressing upwards from one stage to another to the summit of perfection, goodness and beauty – as in Plato's *Symposium*, for example, or in the *Phaedo*; this idea does not generally diverge from the Christian view (and could if necessary be used as a suitable camouflage for something else); but it does differ very sharply from the Christian/Aristotelian concept, which sees man as an objective link in a continuous hierarchical order. The Renaissance thinker, wildly enthusiastic about proportion and science, used Plato's idea as a means of destroying the Christian/feudal hierarchy, and at the same time as a basis for man's independence and his special rights as a rational being.

Plato's second basic idea seemed to the Renaissance thinker to point the way to this goal. It is concerned with methods he recommended, under the influence of the Pythagorean school, in the work he wrote in his old age, the *Timaeus*: he continues with his original distinction between the world of appearances and the actual world; but this time he endeavours to tackle it from the mathematical angle. He already knows that ideas are not simple prototypes, and that they possess a specific *number* of elements which can be determined. Working on this basis, he has a shot at breaking down the multiplicity of reality into its essential components and expressing these components in precise terms. The Renaissance scientist thought of mathematics as the apex of scientific accuracy; he therefore found in Plato's *Timaeus* a justification for his procedural method and arguments against the Christian Aristotelian on the one hand; and on the other hand, it formed the intellectual background against which he could elaborate his demand for precision, together with his view of what science is and what it isn't.

It may seem paradoxical – but the classical scientist who thinks of himself as a materialist, or is thought of as one (which virtually makes him an atheist) thinks along the same lines as Plato the idealist. He thinks in terms of objects, of something which lies outside himself and is in that sense objective. But his thinking is not directed exclusively outwards, he also stands on the opposite side of the fence as a theoretician, a man who *looks*, observes, scrutinizes an object from various different angles; his importance and the effect he achieves result specifically from this narrowing down of human questions into theoretical terms. Being a scientist in the classical sense means dividing reality into (a) objects which can be grasped with the senses and (b) the idea of these objects. The reality of objects includes everything: their nature as an object, man's artificial creations as an object, even man himself as an object among objects. The scientist gets a grip on them if he himself acts purely as a theoretician, if he excludes his own subjective personality as far as possible and becomes anonymous from the human point of view. But this narrowing down also leads to the reduction of the infinitely polymorphous and dynamically variable material world of objects to a relatively small number of characteristic features and lasting benefits. The theoretician expresses this carefully and strictly – preferably in mathematical terms – and in this way finds the corresponding *idea*, which can be rationally reproduced. By this means the concrete reality is severely simplified, becoming easier to control, and in fact becoming more and more certain as the essential, repeatable and reproducible features and their unequivocal expression are made abstract with increasing precision. In this way it is possible to reproduce objects technically as well as intellectually. But this is still only a mechanical process, a question of the correct practical application by technicians skilled in such techniques. Yet the actual constructor who hands man the key which will allow him to gain control of the external world, and formulates the idea of such control, is a theoretician. But this theoretical idea is of its very nature Platonic: it is relieved of dynamic, over-hasty reality (*ex actu*), and reduced to a 'law', to 'matter', 'force', 'impulse', etc.

But at the same time the subjective element is removed from the concrete world as being 'something quite different' – and hence untrustworthy. All that remains of the whole subjective aspect is reason, which is only too sure of itself, or alternatively only too much at variance with itself. Exactly how insecure it is, how much its ostensibly unshakeable preconditions were really prejudices, will become clear later, when it lapses into subjectivism and irrationalism and heralds the bankruptcy of common sense, which is supposed to be so healthy. The efforts made by classical science to simplify things, efforts which embrace the whole of the concrete world, do admittedly achieve some oustanding results; Galileo and Newton construct a new design for the cosmos, seeing it as governed by laws which are stated once and for all. They thus give man the authority to gain technical control over the cosmos. But if we look at it in a radical historical light, all that classical science did was to repeat once again what the classical world had arrived at even before the time of Plato – though on a higher level, with more accomplished rational means and methods and with more accurate measuring instruments. All Aristotle's achievements, his efforts to find a common dimension for man and the cosmos – i.e. the very things which the medieval concept of order was familiar with, although the medieval effort is a crude one – are still alien to classical science. And it is also miles away from the 'hoministic' idea – which originated with Judaism and Jesus – that man is a centre of action, a subjective being surrounded by things. According to the interpretation current in the Renaissance, man is set down in a pre-calculated cosmic space, the intolerable medieval order having just been demolished in this temporal sector. Man is seen from the geometrical angle, as a healthy body with a healthy mind; he is no longer seen as a distorted Gothic figure, faceless, soaring upwards for no apparent reason and then down again, his body lacking all proportion and his mind sunk in darkness. This object-man has just one shortcoming: he lacks the secret challenge of time.

If we look at the problem more carefully and refuse to be carried away by the great achievements of classical science, examining them critically instead, we realize that the Renaissance image of man is reduced to a mere individual, who is extricated from the medieval concept of order and set down in the icy chill of the cosmos; nothing really happens to him there; he is simply at the mercy of fate, and any attempt to reach some other position where he can exert his authority eventually leads to his crashing headlong into an immeasurably vast abyss. Classical humanism is tragic *in that it does not break down these boundaries.*

This, it seems, is the justification for the critical relationship which Pascal had to science and the 'spirit of geometry'. He sees that a knowledge of nature leads man, willingly or unwillingly, to a position of immense loneliness; and he hears his despairing cry echoing unanswered through the cosmos. But he also realizes that the official medieval concept of order is not so very different from the geometrical concept. It, too, is a product of classical antiquity, because it turns God into an object: into something outside the cosmos, infinitely far away from man and infinitely unfamiliar, Plato's concept belongs just as much to classical antiquity as Aristotle's; he does not appreciate the question of man's subjectivism, if we mean by this a creative shaping of human history which helps man to surpass himself both in space *and in time*. So we do not subscribe to the view that the scientific attitude of the Renaissance, which appears on the surface to be diametrically opposed to the medieval, i.e. Aristotelian/Thomist, attitude, differs substantially from it *internally*. If the Renaissance and classical science presented less of a danger to the medieval Church in its struggle to gain a commanding position than the Reformation, this was because, in using the mind and reason as its weapons, it stood outside the Church, whereas the Reformation used real weapons and other material resources inside the Church. The Reformation relied on the Gospel, on the 'true faith' and on Christ, and in this particular historical struggle it was simply more profound in its thinking: this was because its spokesmen, the men who exemplified its teaching, are closer to the prototype of determination which Jesus calls for, to the voice of protest raised in the Apocalypse, and are sustained by the conviction that action is necessary; by this is meant action which is capable of dictating the course of history, which makes allowances for time, and for the temporal modification of everything that the classical/Christian view of space held by the theocratic Church wanted to turn in on itself and deaden.

Pascal is a Protestant inside the Catholic Church; a Protestant who is completely impartial, since he is also a scientist.

His knowledge of nature led him away from the view of man offered by medieval Christianity, and from the idea of a God infinitely far away from man; but this was not the result of the rational arguments put forward by science, which were directed against the religious authorities, but because science put its own views into practice in a logical fashion: men thus saw themselves standing all alone in an empty cosmos. Pascal's thinking doesn't revolve round the visions put forward by the Reformation: it doesn't fade away in Utopian ideas about a fairer world order; nor attempt to make the Church 'cheaper'. Pascal is concerned with establishing what man is, what he is capable of becoming, if his position in the cosmos is really so hopeless, what he should do to give himself some hope of survival – not for himself as an individual, but for the human species, though he knows that he personally will be destroyed by nature.

Pascal's problem is how to preserve and develop humanity in the cosmos; that is his formula for solving the problem of subjective identity.

According to Jesus, the answer lay in a radical decision to perform an act of salvation, an act which allows us to enter tomorrow, not in the sense of everything simply going on as before, of everything being reproduced in a conventional form, but in the sense of the world being governed in a *human manner* and thus becoming worthy of man.

According to Pascal, the answer did not lie in talking about action, but in talking about Jesus. That is his tragedy, and the tragedy of those who come up with the same answer as his.

The ground we have covered so far has led us to two main sources of supply for our own age: (a) classical antiquity and (b) Judaism plus Christianity (or the religion centred on the figure of Jesus). We have witnessed the coming together of these two sources and seen how this transformed them.

Modern man, with two thousand years of Christianity behind him and four hundred years of science, is a humanist by conviction.

He lives on a crest of history: social upheavals and the scientific and technical revolution have offered him the prospect of a new future. We feel very insecure as we look into it. If our humanism is not to become an abstract postulate or a series of conventional and empty phrases, if it is not to be swept away in some crisis or other, we should on no account overlook the fact that we may not back it up solely with force (over nature and over people), nor solely with the idea of Christianity. In themselves these lead only to emptiness and despair. Marxist humanism embraces both of these: the classical world's confidence in rationalism, and in man's proficiency in dealing with objects; and the 'hoministic' challenge echoing down from Judaism in the time of Jesus: to what end will we exercise the authority we have won over space? on behalf of what kind of future? on behalf of which period? how long for?

Now this challenge is already non-religious. It is full of reverence for genuine religious belief, because it knows how it originated and what it is rooted in. But at the same time it is critical of such belief where it finds that Christianity deliberately covers up these roots, either because it is conservative in its outlook, or out of narrow class interests, or because of its reactionary political ambitions, or simply out of intellectual pusillanimity and a primitive attitude to life.

The Marxist is prepared to go along with Christianity provided he finds Christians making an effort to ask radical questions and eager to dig down to the roots of things. He sees in this a hope that they can work together.

So the monuments of Christianity are to the Marxist much more than mute sphinxes.

Footnotes

1) Blaise Pascal: *Pensées*, translated by A. J. Krailsheimer, Penguin, 1966, Fragment 199 (Brunschvicg 72), pp. 88–90.

2) op. cit. Fragment 427 (194), pp. 157–8.

3) op. cit. Fragment 434 (199), p. 165.

4) op. cit. Fragment 407 (465), p. 147.

Part II

THEISM TAKES A LOOK
AT ITSELF

I

THE RELIGIOUS CRISIS —
ONE OF HISTORY'S TRAGEDIES?

1

There was of course an ulterior motive behind our decision to embark on such a detailed study of the great monuments of Christianity.

It won't sound very elevated, but in fact our interest is a *political* one. Firstly, we want to show that we are serious when we talk about the democratic equality enjoyed by all creeds and ideologies in a socialist state — an equality which is completely in tune with the comments made by Marx in his discussion with Bruno Bauer in his pamphlet *The Jewish Question*. Secondly, we are confronted here with absolutely concrete facts connected with the life of the Church, facts which interest us for quite different reasons from those which motivated earlier generations. We cannot fail to react to them. But we want to react properly, as befits a socialist society in the process of maturing. That is why we have decided to dig down to the roots of Christianity. That appears to be the only impartial and unbiased method of obtaining the necessary criteria for making a genuine political distinction. We cannot then continue to devalue this type of politics by calling it degrading: it does not become a tactical manoeuvre which depends in the last analysis on whether or not the Communists are in power. It will be more a policy based on a comprehensive philosophical concept and calling on Marx for support; and in so doing it will openly take into consideration everything which might be even remotely in tune with its own efforts.

What are the procedures in question? What is going on in the Churches? What is their political and spiritual atmosphere like? What type of intellectual or practical activities are being embarked on?

The answers will come more easily if we try to establish how the Christian religion sees itself today. How highly does it rate its hidden inner strength? Where does it see hidden reserves which could be drawn on if necessary? What is its attitude to the facts at issue in the modern world which also find an echo in the Christian Church? How does it rate its own chances as one institution among many worldly institutions?

All this and no doubt many other questions can be summed up in the idea of 'taking a look at itself'. Any movement with social ambitions which fails to take an organized and searching look at itself remains imprisoned by its own past. It loses that living feeling for human and political requirements. But equally it stops being useful for the men and women of today and for the world of politics.

Until recently it seemed that modern Christianity was no longer capable of taking a long look at itself. Externally, everything pointed to this: the churches scrupulously upheld the policies of the powerful capitalist states, down to the tiniest detail. They made no attempt to conceal their firm and militant anti-Communism. They had no desire whatsoever to re-examine any detail in their past, not even those elements which had already been generally discredited. On the spiritual side they stuck rigidly to time-honoured principles which in the circumstances seemed all the pettier for being so venerable.

There is no question that the Churches are now taking a long hard look at themselves; and that consequently there are still powerful sources at work within them to make a regeneration possible. It really is true: God isn't yet dead. One of the most fundamental considerations to be taken into account is the general feeling that the world and religion are both in a critical state. For by far the greater number of Christians, this feeling still takes the form of a causal idea of dependence: the world is going through a crisis *because* religion is going through a crisis.

This leads to new problems which compel Christians to think hard about themselves: mightn't this crisis be triggered off by the backwardness of present-day Christianity? Why couldn't Christianity shake off the challenge of Communism effectively and while there was still time? Why does it seem to have lost the capacity to effect a lasting regeneration? Why did it allow itself to be robbed of the values which, in accordance with its mission, it ought to have defended? What exactly is this mission anyway? What should the Christian's attitude be to non-Christian concepts and projects? What is the significance of modern bourgeois philosophy and sociology to the Christian? What is the significance of Marxism in particular? Or of the non-Christian religious systems which are so widespread in the 'third world'? Which of the cultural, spiritual and material systems of values created by the modern world are acceptable from the Christian point of view? and which of them aren't?

We can find all these questions and many others in contemporary Christian literature. The answers given are by no means unequivocal and authoritative. On the contrary, they are full of dissension and contradictions, full of uneasiness, polemics and a conservative dread of anything new, and full of deep-seated misgivings dating from long ago; they obstinately defend attitudes long since forgotten, and attempt with equal obstinacy to occupy new positions in the new no-man's-land; they vacillate between the two extremes, hesitate before making each move because it might have unforeseeable consequences.

When Christianity takes a look at itself it is setting in motion a political process; its self-examination represents an attempt to inject new life into the forces of Christianity and its authority. It creates uneasiness and agitation after years of inaction.

Is this process an indication that Christianity is going through a crisis? Is there such a thing as a religious crisis? What does the term mean anyway?

2

The religious crisis – we will use this term for the moment, although it is really far too ambiguous – is a far-reaching historical phenomenon. The splitting-up of Christianity – which had originally been a single faith – after the Reformation led to the emergence of a whole series of different denominations: the Protestants, the Calvinists, the Moravian Brethren, the Lutherans and the Anglicans. In the course of the following centuries these denominations split up into even smaller groups, until the whole process ended with a large number of Churches, communities and sects, some important, some unimportant. This progressive disintegration should be seen historically as a sign that Christianity was at this point losing its capacity for working on a universal scale, that it was ceasing to be a sphere of communication between men, as it had been in the Middle Ages.

One essential feature of this crisis is the fact that, starting with the Renaissance, an ever-widening circle of people experienced the Christian religion as something *heteronomous*, irrespective of the methods and subject-matter used to bring them closer to God. There has been a fundamental change. People are no longer gullible enough to put up with having their personal standards and the standards of society in general dictated by revealed truths. In fact the reverse: they begin to feel that rather than being a *law* imprinted by the Creator on to their heart and on to the natural order, the revealed truths are not part of this natural order and are alien to it. And they resist – in some cases with determination, in others with great hesitation and despondency – the social forces which assume the right to direct their day-to-day life and the life of the community of which they form an integral part, by using rules derived from this alien system of laws.

If this sense of the heteronomous state of the Christian revelation and the institution which supplies it spreads – in fact it already almost amounts to a total awareness – this is not the result of a decline in morals or the depravity of human nature, as a devoted pietist might naïvely suppose. Nor is it primarily the result of rational reflection, or a gesture of emancipation by the reason now that it has reached maturity, as a thoughtful liberal would infer. It is more complicated than that. The first impulse does not come either from moral indignation or from the vehemence of a coolly critical mind.

What were the changes which brought about this estrangement between men and the Christian Church?

The economy in kind practised in the Middle Ages, which worked in separate and self-sufficient units and left social relationships to chance, was not in a position to awaken any world-wide interest other than a religious interest. But as soon as trade became part of a system and hence the market came into being, this general meeting-place became the milieu where simple questions were asked and answered, where there was supply and demand, buying and selling, profit and loss – all those elementary economic relationships in which the real, completely unidealized value of the individual is revealed. The self-knowledge people acquired here in the market-place was not marred by a bewildering medley of mysteries and symbols. Instead it gave people insight into their own interests and those of other people and into the way these interests coincide or diverge. This was the beginning of social awareness, and it results in an autonomous generalization: men began to appreciate the enormous importance of a common language used by everybody living anywhere in the country; they also grew aware of the way common customs, time-honoured memories, traditions and cultural values bind men together.

'He is only a Frenchman, my Lord.'
'A Frenchman! Where did you pick up that expression? Are these Burgundians and Bretons and Picards and Gascons beginning to call themselves Frenchmen, just as our fellows are beginning to call themselves Englishmen? They actually talk of France and England as their countries. Theirs, if you please! What is to become of me and you if that way of thinking comes into fashion? ... I can only tell you that it is essentially anti-Catholic and anti-Christian; for the Catholic Church knows only one reality, and that is the realm of Christ's kingdom. Divide that kingdom into nations, and you dethrone Christ. Dethrone Christ, and who will stand between our throats and the sword? The world will perish in the welter of war.' [1]

Shaw, shrewd and ironical, is exaggerating a little here, as usual, but he has managed to express the way Christianity becomes heteronomous, and the outward manifestations of this process, with amazing accuracy.

God is *de trop* in the market-place. But on the battlefield – both in time of war and in the political arena – he becomes a French god, an English god, a German god. An unpleasant, importunate, hateful, outlandish god.

One law which, 'down below' in the market-place, is at first merely a vague fact, something which nobody thinks about, is seized on 'up above', in astronomers' cells, by geometricians, mechanics, opticians and all the other types of craftsmen who are automatically expected to look at things closely, and they immediately begin to think deeply about it: it is the law of reason and autonomy. Later on people read Galileo's *Discorsi* in the market-place, and then all that is left for the Christian faith is an unthinking convention and the tiny bit of room which the Churches know how to hold on to, though they do suffer certain losses all the same.

Admittedly, the situation is not equally pronounced all over Europe, particularly in the classical countries of the Reformation.

Now that the presence of the various Christian Churches had become a sort of foreign body in the towns where the light was gradually dawning, it soon became an equally foreign body in the minds of the bourgeoisie. In their first heroic advance, their awareness of the problem often expressed itself in a radical manner. We hear the cry: God is dead, reason has carried the day! We feel no surprise. The hopes of a class which is fighting to win power like to run ahead of the actual facts of the situation. Right from the beginning of the period of bourgeois revolutions, during the French Revolution in particular, the process of becoming heteronomous continued faster than ever. This makes itself felt in numerical terms in the fact that from the beginning of the nineteenth century onwards the proportion of people who profess the Christian religion in the total population rises in relative terms, but declines all the time in absolute terms. There is absolutely no question today of the Churches being able to implement a large-scale re-Christianization of their former 'possession of souls'. There is a latent religious crisis.

The existence of a religious crisis is also attested by sociology. The far-reaching changes in the demographic structure of both modern capitalist society and socialist society, the way society has been split up, the growing polycentrism, social mobility, a vast number of new and rapid methods of communication, the progressive industrialization of everyday existence – all these different factors have the effect of making the Churches lose their exceptional status in society, so that their capacity to bring men together in communities and integrate them spiritually into these communities is constantly decreasing. The firm solidarity of the religious communities is disappearing. The prestige of the Church communities is at its highest in backward agricultural districts, and in countries where industry is still in its early stages. When these countries, too, have been properly industrialized and have reached a higher rung on the ladder of civilization, the same will happen to their Churches as happened to the Churches in countries where industry has progressed more rapidly and there has been a rise in the standard of living.

Moreover, the situation in which the Churches now find themselves is further complicated by the diverse origins of the various denominations in Europe and the rest of the world. As well as the typical missionary countries, where Christianity is of totally foreign extraction, we also have the countries where either the Catholic or the Protestant faith predominates, with the weaker of the two Churches in a state of *diaspora*, living scattered and in isolation. In countries of mixed religion the two compete with each other and fight a running battle for prestige and power, often under cover but often quite openly as well.

The division of the world into classes, into conflicting socio-economic and ideological systems and political groupings has a crucial effect on the Christian Churches. Their relationship to capitalism and Communism has even had such a far-reaching effect in the last few years that – or so it seems – it has been causing a rift in the Churches and making their position even more precarious. It is not surprising that our contemporaries think of the Churches as worldly organizations, as one group of institutions among many. It is true that there is no lack of research available to show that they do still function efficiently and effectively. People try to calculate whether they are capable of leading men, examine the structure of their cadre, the fighting-power of their leading organs, their elasticity and adaptability, using criteria drawn from the economic world, from production or from public bodies or organizations. The Churches are completely secularized. They are involved in time, trapped in the fight to safeguard their interests.

They succumb to being divided into compartments, a process which affects all the different aspects of their structure; but this also affects the ranks of the faithful; even the statistics given by the Churches themselves have a pretty large permissible variation in their figures showing how many believers there really are. This is where the crisis in religion becomes patently obvious. The piety which formerly showed no sign of discrimination, and therefore made it easy for pastors to carry out their duties, is today full of differences: on the outskirts of their 'flocks' can be found believers who are merely mentioned in the parish-registers and no more – the only sign that they are members of the Church is the symbol of baptism, which at any rate is not visible as a concrete symbol; others who remain effectively out of reach are the non-conformists and 'seasonal' Christians who remember the Church only on special feast-days or for the important events in their life; then there are also 'practising Christians' – the sort who go to Church regularly. Finally, we also have the nucleus of the parish, the lay preachers. The relationship between these different categories varies from parish to parish, from district to district, and according to which denomination has the upper hand in the country concerned. Theologians who do not approve of the sort of self-deception which involves playing about with statistics and are capable of seeing things as they really are admit that Christianity is disappearing in the modern world. They feel that far and away the greater number of believers are women, children and old people. Among people of working age the percentage of church-goers is below average; and religion continues to lose ground, its decline being particularly spectacular in overcrowded industrial towns with a large working class and an influential intelligentsia. Religious faith survives merely as a habit, a tradition, and is tied up with ethnic and social requirements. The memory of it is growing dimmer. This religious crisis covers all the different strata of society, every class, every race and every age-group.

To be sure, the priests do still baptize children; but while the ceremony is being performed the god-parents are thinking that the child might be cold, not that he is in the process of becoming a Christian. Hymns do still ring out in cathedrals; but their spacious interiors are used pathetically little in the course of a day, or even in the course of a year. Hands are still folded in prayer; but genuine

110

piety is becoming increasingly rare. People are still connected to the Church in many ways; but they merely expect practical help in their everyday worries, and when the occasion arises they look for some assurance that they will rest in peace after their death.

The religious crisis is also a phenomenon created by the human psyche. It has a violent effect on the religious values which have been present up to now in man's innermost being, setting the pattern of his life. The conflicts accompanying the crisis are among the most profound that men can experience, but they demand a total reconstruction of one's scale of values, a constant alteration of one's overall attitude to life. So the way in which each person who tackles the problem seriously experiences the religious crisis, and tries to find a means of solving it, is quite exceptionally important to mankind in general.

Christianity without a halo; at the mercy of the autonomous demands of this world. And of its judgement.

3

How does this crisis in Christianity manifest itself?

We intend to reject as inappropriate the narrow-mindedly empirical or pietistic interpretations which can understand the religious crisis only from the point of view of prestige or political expediency. We are concerned with offering an interpretation which will be in keeping with the historical scale of the problem and at the same time theologically acceptable, for this is the only type of interpretation which can really be a determining factor for the historical activity of the various Christian Churches. In so doing we will limit ourselves to the Roman Catholic Church and discover two fundamental ways of looking at things.

The first of these, although formulated as early as the middle of the thirties, can be seen as a typical example of the mentality which has not yet lost its decisive influence in the Catholic Church. The second has been gradually evolving since the beginning of the fifties and will clearly continue to develop. We shall now take a look at both of these attitudes.

Jacques Maritain sees the historical process of the religious crisis as a tragedy of recent history, the tragedy of humanism. The early years of the Middle Ages and the high medieval period are for him the heroic age of man. Medieval man was totally involved with God and his worldly existence was of little importance. When he thought about himself, he always saw himself as God's creature. This undiscriminating religious self-confidence began to disintegrate with the arrival of individualism: admittedly men were still prepared to do penance in God's sight, but they were no longer prepared to do so in the sight of their fellow-men. Now when the autonomy of their own reason began to set the tone of their existence, with no more thought of revealed truths, their whole being, which had originally been totally undivided, was split into two; one half of them constantly felt that it was about to be swallowed up by nature, while the other half struggled in vain to find itself and to credit itself with being of value once again.

So the outcome is a tragic mix-up: the type of humanism which had God as its centre becomes a different type of humanism with man as its centre, but at the same time it somehow loses the real human dimensions. If, says Maritain, this can still be considered as a type of humanism, it deserves the label 'inhuman'. Proof of this can be seen in later developments. 'Man in his dignity', as seen by Rousseau, crumbles away: Darwin reduces him to his basic animal needs, Freud makes him subject to the constraints of his instincts. The upshot of all this is that man's personality comes to an end; this is confirmed when Marx and Communism make their appearance: quite apart from being abolished, the human personality now becomes the property of the state and the collectivist system, being totally absorbed in them.

But equally, continues Maritain, we have here a cultural tragedy. It might still have been possible to detect a Christian element in the Renaissance period, even if such an element had already been naturalized. But the following centuries got rid of Christianity in its entirety. Intelligence and technology – the twin monuments of bourgeois culture – were in control. Man was suppressed. The moments when man is truly himself became increasingly rare.

According to Maritain, both these tragedies end in the tragedy of God. First of all, in the work of Spinoza, Descartes and Malebranche, this affects the principle of transcendency. Geometric reasoning rebels against the divine mystery. Then Hegel transforms the transcendental God into a mere idea, and eventually Nietzsche announces that God is dead. Anyway, how could he live in a world in which his replica – the human personality – has disappeared? Atheism becomes intelligible as an expression of the venom felt by men who have been let down by a society which has failed to remain true to its human mission.

If this imminent historical tragedy is to be averted, Maritain thinks it imperative that God should be the centre of man's existence once again. We must create the necessary conditions on earth so that God can descend from Heaven and man can rise above his own position in the direction of God.

But what will happen to the social situation as it now stands? What will happen to the state as it now is? – after all, its bourgeois structure has become dualistic and it is splitting man in two. It is quite clear, declares Maritain, that it must be destroyed. The Christian agrees with the Communist on this point. But he differs from him in rejecting his purely external, mechanical solution, his revolutionary activity. The Christian knows only one authoritative way to eliminate this alienating dualism: this involves a personal integration of his inner self, the promotion of his spiritual life, the formation of his creative personality, which is religious in this sense. In practical terms this means that the Christian is duty bound to fit economics and politics into an ethical system, and to take an active part in this system as a Christian. That's what being holy, new-style, is, and the absolutely basic mission of the Church consists of fostering this new style of piety, creating it and supporting it. It presents the Christian with a historically powerful ideal which is quite different from the medieval ideal – the latter being dead and gone beyond recall. Even though the typical features of this ideal cannot be determined with any degree of precision, Maritain is none the less convinced that they are so expressive that it would be possible to make a practical effort to acquire them. The new society which is to emerge cannot be the homogeneous structure of the Middle Ages, which was ordered 'from above'; instead it is a pluralistic structure in which the forces of the collective, of groups and individuals, mutually support and complement each other. So its economic system should, for instance, include an agriculture based on the family unit as well as a collectivized industrial system; it will still be based on private ownership, even if this is used for the common good; economic life takes place within a structure made up of corporations, the corporations serving production being subordinate to the consumer corporations, which in their turn are subordinate to the political corporations. In the legal sphere this type of society will take the differences between the different groups and their various rights and duties into consideration, always remembering to keep the general Christian goal in sight. In the political field the prevailing note will be tolerance, tolerance guided by the Christian spirit; this Christian spirit must become a leading political authority taking care of the business of training up elites to occupy key positions.

According to Maritain, this new society with its Christian orientation cannot grow up on the foundations of bourgeois society, since it is too egoistic and individualistic. But nor can it come into being in accordance with the Messianic-cum-collectivist ideas put forward by the Communists. Maritain thinks we can steer a middle course between these two extremes by adopting a Christian and personalistic solution, a reconciliation between man and nature, civilization and culture, in other words: God. In his book *Humanisme intégral* (1936) he states that this historical Christian ideal cannot be realized in its entirety until capitalism has been overthrown. Now we should not overestimate this statement. It is clear from the context that it contains nothing more than the plea that capitalist society should be cleansed of its bourgeois elements; it is therefore essentially exactly the same as what is labelled 'Christian democracy' in the social and political philosophy of Thomism.

After the Second World War, i.e. from the beginning of the fifties onwards, a new way of looking at the religious crisis arose in Catholic theological circles, one which looked a lot more level-headed.

The French Jesuit Desqueyrat [2] sees the religious crisis as a crisis on a universal, world-wide scale, affecting not merely the Christian religion, but religion in general; it is not just a question of religion deteriorating from civilized formulae to less civilized ones, but of non-belief growing deeper all the time. But Desqueyrat does not think of this tragic collapse as being expressly religious and petering out purely and simply in the question of what will become of Christianity and the Christian Churches in the future. He sees it rather as a symptom of a general uprooting created by a far-reaching and violent revolution. Hence it is not that religion or Christianity is going through a period of crisis, but that this all-pervading revolution represents a planetary crisis among the men of today.

We must understand the historical significance of this revolutionary process, which affects the whole world – that is the task which faces Christianity today. There is therefore no point in measuring this revolution by the standards of European history and the European mind; we will scarcely be able to proceed by taking our models from the classical period of Christianity. Desqueyrat is convinced that if Christianity is not to become purely an affair of insignificant, socially isolated elites, it must throw its doors open to the world at large, and make an effort to gain a foothold in the other great world cultures as well as in the cultures of the West – i.e. in India, China and Africa. It must become the champion of revolutionary mysticism.

What a frightful expression that is! But Desqueyrat does not use it to mean some religious credo or other. He thinks of it as a philosophy concerned with man and the world, and if necessary with God as well, if men ask such questions at all; it is a scale of values and a programme of activity. It tells us, concludes Desqueyrat, why and how a 'human' universe should be organized.

The world of today is completely under the spell of science and the cult of objectivity; but according to Desqueyrat, it should not be allowed to fall into the clutches of positivism. On the contrary, it must always leave an increasingly large amount of room for what modern philosophers call the 'irrational'. In the modern world people look for ways of deriving as much benefit as possible from every aspect of life; the revolution will force people to make sure that this attitude does not deteriorate into a banal type of utilitarianism, but instead devotes its creative strength to everyday existence. Even the new reality will not put an end to mass-production, but this does not mean that it will lead to people becoming stereotyped. Man is not a passive product of history, but rather a history which produces itself; in other words, he is activity. Desqueyrat draws immensely far-reaching practical conclusions from these observations; the mind reduces the scope of individual or social determinism; as it does so, the 'holy ones' are called on to open wide the doors of history as a whole and the history of religion in particular.

We can see at first glance that this interpretation of the religious crisis differs sharply from Maritain's view. Whereas Maritain thinks of our age as a progressive process of decay, and of Communism as the end-product of this historical disintegration, Desqueyrat, realizing that the revolution is being played out on a universal and planetary scale, sees it as an autonomous process which is painfully giving birth to a new world. Nothing is complete; everything in which and by which we live challenges us. The Christian is a man who knows how to react with feeling, who has a keen understanding of the spiritual scale of the revolution, of its mysticism.

This way of looking at our age and the religious crisis gained ground during the fifties, although for the time being it was restricted to fairly exclusive theological circles. It was not until the beginning of the sixties that it began to look like a more practical proposition with greater potential.

We are now familiar with two different interpretations of the religious crisis, both of them theologically relevant.

The first of these is the Thomist interpretation; it is peculiar to the closed circle of Catholicism.

The second interpretation is non-Thomist; it embodies the concept of an open type of Christianity. The conflict between the two has already been settled in principle. But in practice, it will be with us for a long time yet.

Footnotes

1) George Bernard Shaw: *St Joan*, Scene IV.
2) R. P. A. Desqueyrat s.j.: *La Crise religieuse des temps nouveaux*, Paris, 1955.

2

UNIVERSALITY
AND PARTICULARITY

1

Understanding is the first step towards overcoming.

Contemporary Christianity often aroused the antagonism of progressive groups and classes – it still does so in fact – by being linked to the interests of the *grande bourgeoisie*.

We shall now make a careful analysis of this situation; it is true that it will do nothing to alter our verdict that we must do our utmost to eliminate what is known as 'integralism', the subordination of all secular life to Christianity, from social and political life. But unlike criticisms motivated more by instinctive aversion than by a careful consideration of the facts, this type of study can help to create new motivations: it can lay bare the surface of the fundamental social problems which confront every large-scale movement with any degree of self-awareness in our modern world – this applies, for instance, to Catholicism, but equally well to Communism; and it can help us to understand what the Church thought about these problems; how it proceeded to solve them; why it chose the solution it did; and why exactly this solution is so vulnerable and hopeless.

By proceeding in this way, we will ask ourselves certain questions about our own ideas, concepts and plans.

2

The Thomist theory of Catholicism starts out from what is known as 'political Catholicism' or 'Integralism'; this was an attempt to solve the old problem of man's universality.

If we want to express this word in extremely general terms, we can think of it as an abstract cipher comprising everything that we can classify as the generic characteristics of the human race. Man is naturally indivisible; if we look at him from the outside, he appears to be a creature capable of adapting himself to a universal scale; nowadays we are even attempting to adapt ourselves to a cosmic scale or, more accurately, to an interplanetary scale. Seen from the inside he appears to be phylogenically definitive and to have had his limits fixed once and for all in relation to the whole of non-human nature. But over and above this, universality clearly signifies the indivisibility of the human element in man with reference to himself: we cannot contemplate man in terms of 'more' or 'less' unless we want to finish up with the atrocities of genocide. Man is also a limiting value for himself. This concept includes the criterion which decides him to direct his whole nature outwards (to be extrovert) and in so doing to go beyond himself (to transcend himself). We refer to his capacity to give everything a human stamp, to impart human features to everything he touches.

Universality is therefore within man's power; it is constantly being developed and is capable of arousing dormant and lethargic nature to self-awareness, transforming it from a mere existence governed by a causal relationship to an end in itself. While man exhausts in himself the indifference with which he views himself as a man, the indifference and coldness of nature towards the human race is also exhausted. This universality finds an elementary and practical expression in the social yield, with the help of which man *becomes* a universal being. The universality of the human race asserts itself historically as a process whose success is never more than partial, particular and incomplete, a process made up of alternating acts of sovereignty and dominion. So each living force in society (each group, social class or movement) which possesses a marked sense of its responsibility attempts to realize its plans and ideas for man as a social being on a universal scale. But as soon as they begin to think of their scheme as definitive, a masterpiece of perfection, they cut themselves off and in the concrete course of history will be seen as no more than a partial phenomenon which has been exploded.

Admittedly, this does not mean that, in exploding the overall concept, we might not be able to retain some elements which are worth bearing in mind and studying creatively.

I see the contribution made by Christianity as it developed in the time of Jesus as the fact that, in opposition to the cosmopolitan concept of the Roman Empire, whose structure was quite clearly made up of separate sections at that time, it claimed that man must once again be interpreted generically. I have called this 'revelation' the 'hominism' of the age of Jesus: its aim was to fit man into a web, so that he could find the generic place where he belonged as a member of the human race; it objects to the 'instrumental' theory which sees man as a slave, a mere tool, and sets the limits within which his generic value should be recognized in the widest sense of the term.

Admittedly, Christian hominism has only been able to do this in a fragmentary fashion, with the help of images, symbols and myths.

The new Christian era under Constantine gave the men of the Church a golden opportunity: they made it a point of honour to turn the Church into a universal institution capable of bringing men together, and using long-term obligations to create a social order which would be worthy of the human race.

The Church has never succeeded in putting the finishing touches to this project, but nor has it ever abandoned the idea altogether. It is always trying to construct the perfect society. Thomism represents one of the high-points in this series of attempts.

It is to Marx's credit that he took up Hegel's findings, studied them critically, and found a way of formulating the problem of man's universality by voicing the idea that history is a natural process, and that up to now the course of history has been chiefly a history of class warfare. This idea would not in itself exclude a Utopian solution to the problem. Marx's contribution was to show that the capitalist method of production was the first method to convert the universe of values, including that of man, into commodities; that it created an international market; and that in so doing it brought about the objective unification of the world, or at any rate of the world as an object of selfish class interest. So in capitalism there emerged for the first time in history a *real* possibility of realizing man's indivisibility – on the basic of economic unification. But the invariable precondition is that the particular and particularizing circumstances must be overcome. For this reason – and not because he holds some sort of Messianic view – Marx sees the proletariat as the only *part* of society capable of winning the honorary title 'man'. Nature being made human, man being made natural, industry as the true historical nature of man, class warfare – these are the nodal points in the process of emancipation which is to free man as a universally valid being from his position within the many different sections of history.

But because of its Thomist orientation, the Church sees the whole process in a different light. It doesn't seize on the *progressive* aspect of the new universality of the economic world as initiated by the bourgeoisie; it sees this merely as an increasingly deep-seated process of disintegration, as an unprecedented disruption of order.

The Thomists see the bourgeois humanism whose spiritual ambience is the background to this process as the exact opposite of the hoministic challenge offered by Christianity. We have here the beginnings of a process within the Catholic Church which culminates in a plan to set up a renewal of order, in opposition to the lack of order of the bourgeoisie. A bold attempt, but it is a losing battle right from the outset, considering the historical dimensions of the problem.

3

In the 1870s the Roman Catholic Church was compelled by the course of events to adopt a form of political realism; this in fact resulted in a do-or-die situation for the Church. Those princes of the Church who reflected soberly on the situation knew that to cling to their theocratic powers would be sheer senile obstinacy; that this would only lead to the emergence of disastrous radical currents inside the Church; and that it was essential that they should take great pains to evolve a plan which would be Christian and yet could hope to be effective in this world as well. The Church began work on this plan in the 1870s, when Pope Leo XIII (1878–1903) ascended the papal throne.

If we study these facts carefully, it becomes clear that the fact that the Vatican gradually became a capitalist property-owner in its own right was not of vital importance. The ways in which it proceeded to amass capital are certainly important from the point of view of its immediate day-to-day policy, but they do not seriously affect the far-sighted political schema which was now being prepared. Criticism which merely makes a revealing comparison between the general Christian ideals and the concrete business of amassing capital inside the Churches overlooks something much more serious; the new plan for creating universality in the Christian Churches is vitally important for the *overall* policy of the Roman Catholic Church in the long and highly eventful period from 1900 to 1950. The preparatory work for this schema lasted from the beginning of the 1880s to the middle of the '90s; by then its basic outline had been established on the basis of several totally independent surveys. Several more concrete versions were devised in the following decades, but none of the original ideas was altered in any way.

The various surveys took the philosophical principles of Thomism as their starting-point, going on from there to a socio-political doctrine, and finishing by formulating the principles for setting up and organizing a practical Christian policy.

4

The philosophical data for the scheme are set out in the encyclical *Aeterni Patris* (1879) and elaborated in the encyclicals *De Libertate* (1888) and *Rerum novarum* (1891). They call for a revival of Thomism; and this meant that Thomism was once again used in the Church, now that its eternal validity had been ratified. Conversely, Thomist critics concluded that the disintegration of bourgeois philosophy was merely a reflection of the initial transformation of what had once been order into disorder. The Renaissance – *the sins of the Italians* – did not become a danger because of the turning-point it reached with Copernicus, but because of its atomizing attitude derived from Ionic philosophy; thanks to this attitude reason could begin – though in a very small way – to think of itself as possessing mastery over objects. The Reformation – *the sins of the Germans* – made the authority of belief and theology relative. Thus the way was paved for modern rationalism, which progressed via Descartes, the French Enlightenment philosophers and Kant, eventually ending in the abstract ideas of *reason*, science, progress and civilization – those idols of a new age. On the threshold of the 1880s even the Thomists realized how much their ideas had been caricatured.

The Thomist critique of bourgeois rationalism hits the nail on the head when it asks the following question: why should human reason be thought of as the highest and ultimate authority, when it is in fact quite clear that the statements made by reason are also at the mercy of contingency?

Such questions were no longer new, and had not been so ever since the time of Hegel. But the Thomists drew some far-reaching critical conclusions from them which were at the same time constructive. They addressed themselves chiefly to their own people: they criticized Christian Scholasticism for having become too academic. They preached a return to a state where reason still relied on the absolute authority of God; they wanted reason to revise its activity in such a way that it could grasp what God's objective intentions were and thus become the *intellect* of belief. The new version of Thomism was heralded as the philosophy of an intellectual elite within the Catholic Church, a philosophy capable of looking further and deeper, beyond the gloomy surface of routine conflicts and conflicting interests, and therefore also equipped to operate on a practical level.

That is why the Church fiercely resisted all attempts to obtain a new impetus to Christian thinking from bourgeois philosophy; such attempts were being made among Catholic intellectuals at the beginning of the twentieth century, and they were rejected by the ecclesiastical authorities in their anti-modernistic encyclicals. Modernism has one negative principle – it wishes to bar the claim that belief must be absolute from science and history; but this would condemn the Church to a tacit recognition of the autonomy of science and compel it to adhere to a sterile policy; by means of its positive principle it restricts the function of belief to man's inner life, to existential experiences: this gives it an irrational ring, which logically makes it seem anti-intellectual.

Thomism, on the other hand, wishes to be a philosophy and an ideology with the whole vast, world-wide institution of the Church at its disposal, and at the same time aims to have enough worldly power to make effective action feasible.

In the social domain Thomism pits the ideal of an objective order against the rationalistic free will of bourgeois philosophy; this objective order is indicated by means of irrevocable laws, which allot each person and each object its own special place and special function in the hierarchical structure of the Kingdom of God. Bourgeois rationalism refused to recognize this and that was, according to the Thomists, the beginning of the catastrophe.

For, when once man is firmly persuaded that he is subject to no one, it follows that the efficient cause of the unity of civil society is not to be sought, in any principle external to man, or superior to him, but simply in the free-will of individuals; that the authority of the State comes from the people only; and that, just as every man's individual reason is his only rule of life, so the collective reason of the community should be the supreme guide in the management of all public affairs. Hence the doctrine of the supremacy of the greatest number, and that all right and duty reside in the majority.[1]

But in the opinion of the ecclesiastical authorities this is where all yardsticks for judging good and bad disappear. Everyone is allowed to do what he wants. The ordinary mass of people, who rely on an imaginary sovereignty, have a permanent liking for disturbances and rebellions. '*Quod satis testatur dimicatio propemodum quotidiana contra Socialistas*,' remarks Leo XIII in a marginal note.

The Thomists' criticism of the liberalism of the bourgeoisie is devastating indeed – and at bottom perfectly justified. The inference it draws from this is again radically clear-cut: both in theory and in practice we must do away with the *principle* of a democratic syphoning-off of the power of the state (though this does not preclude fighting for the freedom offered by democracy). This principle is to be replaced by another: that of state-sovereignty, which is to be accepted as an objective and authoritative power.

But problems begin to crop up here for the socio-political doctrine put forward by the Thomists. The cardinal question concerns its relationship to the proletariat, to the labour movement and to Marxism.

The most common criticisms levelled at the socio-political doctrine of the Roman Catholic Church are restricted in the main to reproaching it for being scientifically untenable and for the reactionary and dogmatic nature of its aims. As if that were the most important aspect of the question! The scheme put forward by the Thomists is concerned with something quite different from simple demagogy, which any worker would be capable of seeing through, even if he were only slightly class-conscious. What they want to do is to construct a system of interconnecting links whose aim is to fit the proletariat into the power system.

The Church feels that the following steps are necessary in order to achieve this: on the theoretical side, all the prejudices inherent in bourgeois rationalism must be got rid of in all their various forms; on the practical side, political liberalism must be destroyed, and there must be a return to the principles of the 'organic interpretation of society'. If this succeeds, the Church is convinced that their Marxist and Socialist critics will have the ground cut from under their feet. After all, Socialism, Communism, and Marxism are nothing if seen as products of the disintegration of the *bourgeoisie* carried to extremes, as the most shocking of all bourgeois heresies, because they invalidate such natural human obligations as private ownership, and at the same time abrogate the very foundation of such obligations – religion. If society is not to collapse altogether under the onslaught of the Communists – which the Thomists see as the ultimate phase of the disintegration of the bourgeoisie, since the only possible sequel is chaos – the working classes must be integrated into the system of authority. The necessary prerequisites for integration are: a sound Christian social doctrine – it is the Church's task to see that it is properly disseminated; the basic principles of this doctrine must be fitted into the state legislature and executive; co-operative associations, corporations and organizations must be imbued with its spirit, and these will implement social justice by balancing the different interests involved against each other. This would lead to the emergence of a social organism based on the innate functional inequality of men and it is this which will ensure that the social balance is maintained. The ideal task of the state is the creation and maintenance of the necessary legal preconditions, and it would also have to guarantee that the functional sovereignty of the various different parts of this organic whole is not violated, that it is not influenced or unnecessarily interfered with, as long as it does not exceed its appointed limits. The task of the Churches and the Christians is to co-operate in this constructive social activity and cultivate an awareness that it is morally binding. Admittedly, the resulting social order will not be a *bourgeois* democracy any more, but a *Christian* one, deriving its support from God and the binding relationship between man and God, and apportioning a certain measure of freedom in his social life to each member of society. But this freedom is no longer to be understood in the same way as the *bourgeoisie* understood it, either in its individualistic (liberalistic) form or in its collectivist (which the Church later expressed in concrete terms as Fascist or Communist) form.

There is a very deliberate shift of emphasis in these objective relationships in Thomism. When the Thomist makes a critical and constructive approach to the period in which history has become universal, he overlooks the fact that the hundred-year period in which the world has gradually been secularized has seen the emergence of a policy which has proved to be one of concentrated economy. Thomism is therefore working out theoretical attempts aimed at making politics sacred, so that class differences can disappear in an abstract communion of interests throughout the whole social organism.

This model for a Christian democratic regime invites comparison with the social order which Marx called a 'democracy of serfdom', because the life of the people and the life of the state merge into each other, resulting in total alienation.

5

By describing the Thomists' scheme in these terms we do not wish to give the impression that we consider it a wild idea in theory and a feeble idea in practice.

Christian democracy has been operating as a mass movement from the beginning of the twentieth century. It grew in the decades between the two wars and then began to branch out in a distinctive way after the Second World War.

The building policy of the international and national Catholic organizations, institutions and institutes (and their Protestant counterparts) is thoroughly functional and makes itself felt right down to the tiniest details of life in society. Its organization is first-class; it is generally controlled by an elite and it has adequate material resources. It has its political *avant-garde* on the worldly plane in the Christian-Democrat parties. In Europe these were or are the champions of the idea of creating a united Christian Europe. Equally important is the part they play in the political life of several of the developing countries. We should also think of the Federal Republic of Germany in this context, for in its constitution the theoretical scheme we have been discussing has been as it were transferred into the legal sphere.

If we want to make a detailed critical assessment of the Thomists' scheme, we should not be satisfied with a mere 'theoretical refu-tation' or a constant 'policy of exposure' which involves unearthing its reactionary entrails – which is what often happens in certain 'popular Marxist' works. On the contrary, we must even go as far as to confirm that it looks squarely at the negative symptoms – not at the causes – of the disintegration of the bourgeoisie, and does so accurately and with considerable insight. From the religious angle, however, it makes this one aspect of the process of disintegration absolute. One of the consequences of this – and this is also its most striking feature – is its institutionalized anti-Communism, which is utterly different from bourgeois anti-Communism.

Further, we must state that the Thomists' blueprint does cor-respond to one of the real needs of mankind – after the terrible lessons they have been taught by history, men are already at least partly aware of their indivisibility, and they feel in need of an order in which they *could* emancipate themselves as members of the human race, and establish and consolidate their species. But the original draft of this order, and later on the final schema as outlined in the Thomist plan, relates to a situation which existed before modern man began to become universal, thanks to the new production methods being introduced. So this means that it understands nothing of the dynamic force behind this process. It is true that the prototype is made out to be universal, but the only way for it to be realized is for the bourgeoisie to get hold of it and make it particular rather than universal. This is what has been happening ever since the prototype was first formulated, tentatively at first, with an elementary attempt from time to time, but later on, particularly after the Second World War, it has been happening quite deliberately.

That is the ominous paradox of the Thomist schema. The Thomists are always trying to find some way round the difficulty. But they are always getting themselves entangled all over again.

A close study of Thomism and its plan for a Christian democracy is highly instructive. It confronts us with a large number of questions: on what basis can we construct a human order which would be genuinely universal in scope? How far can Marxism go in throwing itself open, in order to win over men and bring them together, without losing face in these long-drawn-out negotiations? What in fact is the real heart of the Communist programme, if we choose to understand this as a programme whose aim is to set up an order based on universal human freedom?

Our adversary can always prompt us with the answers.

Footnote

1) Encyclical by Pope Leo XIII: *De Libertate*, June 1888; English translation published by the Catholic Truth Society in *The Pope and the People: Select Letters and Addresses by Pope Leo XIII on Social Questions*, 1903.

3

THEOLOGY AND MODERN MAN

1

Those theologians who know something of the ominous paradox of Thomism are still in the minority so far. But they are the leavening element in contemporary Christianity.

Theologians! What possible use are they in a world which has now reached the parting of the ways? What can theology possibly mean to modern man anyway?

How exactly do we conceive of theology?

The main point is that many people are convinced that theology has nothing to do with science. The science of God – a blatant contradiction in terms, surely? That's how it seems to the materialist, to the positivist, and to a considerable number of subjective and objective idealists.

As a rule they think of theology as a perverted, systematic intellectual exercise, both in its content and in its method.

How can one seriously go into ontological or non-ontological evidence of the existence of God? What is the cult of Christ and the cult of the Virgin Mary all about, if it is not even certain that Jesus really existed as a historical figure, so that the question of whether or not his mother was ever alive must also remain open? What kind of practical significance can there possibly be in a doctrine all about angels and demons? What was Christ's opinion of himself? Did he realize that he is God?

Theologians, too, sometimes dig as deep as this in their reflections.

But, as usual, the whole question is more complicated than that.

Admittedly, theology cannot be counted as one of the exact sciences, nor as philosophy, in that philosophy deals exclusively with objects. The principal subject-matter of theology is a series of intellectual fictions. In this respect it is unscientific. But this does not mean that theological pronouncements are automatically meaningless, and that the theologians' thinking (at this point theology coincides to a certain extent with the intellectual methods used by scientists and philosophers) is incapable of making observations in any one specific field.

The fact is that even the most confused fabrication is a product of the human mind, and even in this form it still represents a statement made by man about himself; it can even indicate that some historical crossroads have been arrived at, if we examine it carefully.

Every system of theological pronouncements – and this again is true of every philosophy – is a child of its age, embracing in its own particular way the problems, hopes, antipathies, concrete worries and fabrications of its period. The mere fact that the majority of contemporary theologians rely on dogmas, i.e. on intellectual constants which they accept unreservedly and uncritically, does not exclude the possibility that theology, too, will develop. If we examine the objective causes and subjective motives underlying this type of development, we will be in a position to appreciate what exactly the Churches think of themselves, what questions they are pondering and how, what type of suggestions they are making, what their aims are, what this activity or that really signifies.

Theology is an intellectual instrument for a cultural belief; it is an articulate belief in God which is intellectually and spiritually under control. In this respect it is as much a product of culture as art or philosophy. Just as with art and philosophy, it reflects the various eras through which it has passed, those eras which have influenced it and been influenced by it. From this point of view, a critical and impartial study of the history of theology can come up with opinions which are just as significant as those obtained through a study of history, philosophy, art or science.

Admittedly, theology does differ considerably from other types of intellectual or spiritual reflection in that it drags the polar tension between God and man into everything, every object it gets its hands on, or – if we want to put it another way – it expresses everything according to the reference system relative/absolute, temporal/

eternal, finite/infinite. According to the theologians' way of thinking, these are diametrical opposites. It is not in man's power to bridge the gulf between them; that is up to God. In this concept of God, theology introduces an element of mystery, and this has a decisive influence on its significance.

But by aligning all its subject-matter so that it comes into the field of force of this fictitious polarity, theology arrives at an attitude which allows it a high degree of abstraction. God becomes a medium which makes everything seem transitory and impermanent: everything turns out to be 'slight'. This means that the theologian is never in direct contact with anything: he always keeps his hands clean. Yet on the other hand, we should not think of theology as set in its ways or rigid. Theologians dwell in a world of fantasy, and this can easily lead them to think that 'slight' equals 'nothing': they keep their gaze fixed on God and on God alone. But they can equally well turn their attention to man, in an attitude full of understanding, compassion and love: in that case 'slight' becomes a call for 'more'. Their theology takes on an anthropological note. At any rate: God the medium can perhaps provide the necessary impetus for *cultured* theologians to indulge in grandiose reflections, but he can equally well lead to gloomy narrow-mindedness. He can impart that inner peace without which no genuine action can be accomplished, but he can also lead to smug inflexibility. This can be the key which prevents the Christian entering the world once and for all; but it can also open wide the door leading into the world.

2

One other theological movement is also a direct result of the religious crisis. But the way in which its adherents interpret the crisis and the questions they ask in so doing are very different – one might even say, diametrically different – from the traditional theological view. It is of course true that they, too, think of the Christian faith as being something of fundamental value, but they do not see the religious crisis as a historical tragedy. They reflect diligently on the historical facts with which conservative theology is also concerned; but they do not see these as signifying a progressive process of disintegration, snowballing in a menacing fashion. They, too, think of the Church as the indelible seal imprinted on history by Christ; but they are aware that the Church is a temporal institution, and so do not glorify all that it does without reservation. Being a Christian is to them the highest honour men can achieve; yet they see no reason why one individual should profess publicly that he is a Christian, lay claim to this particular title as exclusively his, and turn it into a sectarian matter. They, too, are universalistic; but they have a more highly developed feeling for time and for the modifications caused by time than for spatial structure. They reflect certain specific tendencies of our age with great sympathy and understanding. The people who initiated this particular branch of theology, and those who now champion it, are not, it is true, a large group, but they are important from the intellectual point of view and, in the last analysis, from the practical angle, though admittedly they do lack a firm focus.

The names of Edouard Mounier, Gabriel Marcel, Pierre Teilhard de Chardin, Marie-Dominique Chenu, Johannes B. Metz, Karl Rahner, Romano Guardi, Hans Küng and a whole lot of others are already beginning to ring as momentously in the Catholic Church of today as those of their counterparts in the Protestant Church: Karl Barth, Friedrich Gogarten, Rudolf Bultmann, Josef L. Hromádka, Paul Tillich and a growing number of German, Anglo-Saxon and Scandinavian theologians. Our discussions have dealt with Catholicism up to now, so let us stick to this policy, partly for the sake of conciseness, but also because the new theol
gcial outlook among Catholics has its own particular stamp.

3

The central motif which runs through this theological outlook, giving it its dynamic diameter, is the *time* aspect and, closely bound up with this, the element of *hope*, which is so significant from the subjective point of view. Now there is nothing specially new about that, in the consciousness of an age packed with upheavals; but that theologians should choose to adopt this outlook is a really radical change.

The new theological attitude accounts chiefly for the fact that modern man has little understanding of the 'perfections' of past centuries and the social systems of the past. Its adherents do not think of the 'golden age' as having occurred in some archaic period in remote antiquity – but nor do they place it in the recent past. They think of the past as over and done with for good. The future, on the other hand, is a reality which is not yet with us and which – and this is crucial – has never been with us so far. Our attitude to the future cannot be theoretical, but must be active, operational and practical. For the man of today the future does not represent a task imposed on him by someone, but a *breakthrough* which he is to accomplish, in the wake of which a new civilization will arise, a civilization which is his own work, the work of man. He sees time as the realm in which he and he alone can act by means of gestures and gesticulations. He is to create in the future an artificial world of a new quality, an *artificium* in which mankind will at last feel at home on earth. Modern theologians have their eyes open to this changed spiritual environment, and they observe that they are confronted by a whole series of questions on which theologians have long been silent – or if they have taken them up, they have done so very cautiously, distorting them wildly.

In the first place, they turn their attention to the historical attitude which judges the civilizing process set in motion by the Renaissance solely on its negative characteristics. As long as the emphasis was placed on this aspect, it was impossible for modern theologians to get to work, according to Marie-Dominique Chenu. And today we are indeed witnessing the appearance of a tragic paradox in Christianity: we have a theology of war, a theology of trade relations, a theology of history, but Christianity has never dealt with the question of labour and tried to produce something theologically relevant. Chenu thinks that this shocking omission is a result of the Church's conservative attitude, which made it incapable of making a dispassionate appraisal of the progressive aspects of the process of civilization; the result was that the Church saw the problem as something outside its own sphere, and reacted to it as if this really were the case.

It did not fancy the idea of machines, and had no understanding for the proletariat; these two factors combined to make it a staunch upholder of conservative ideals: craftsmen's workshops, patriarchal families, small-scale private ownership and self-sufficient peasantry. Because the Church clung to the good old days, so did theology. And since theology clung to the good old days, so did the Church.

This meant that those elements which men needed in order to be able to take stock of themselves afresh flourished elsewhere, outside the Church and in opposition to it: in the proletariat. The Church must take the blame for the atheism of the proletariat, says Chenu. Any theological examination capable of freeing the Church from the claims which imprison it in the past, and at the same time able to inject new energy into it, must therefore – according to Chenu – start from the question of what man is, what his relationship is to nature, and what sort of order forms the framework for this relationship. The new-style theologians will no longer make do with the idea that man is a creature endowed with the gift of reason; what is more important is that he is himself a creator, an *artifex*.

If we take this as a purely abstract view it has nothing new to say: man always was creative. But the historical process which we mentioned earlier has changed the emphasis; now the most important characteristic of man is the fact that he is productive. Chenu points out [1] the importance of technological development even in the Middle Ages. The material and clerical hold of feudalism was broken by new means of transport, the result of introducing harness and horseshoe, which led to a much wider circulation of agricultural produce and greater mobility of population. Similarly the technological development that has brought into being the modern age in Europe, though depending on the creation of a proletariat with all its attendant misery, is in itself, according to Chenu, a liberating influence. For it has produced social ownership, and continues to do so to an accelerating extent. This means that production will no longer put up with individuals aiming at personal gain, whether or not this satisfies the worker's basic requirements for subsistence or the capitalist's expectations of profit. Production is run on objective lines, and aims to create a community which rids men of their individual interests. Hence a theology of labour cannot restrict its criticism of capitalism to demanding a reasonable limit to the amount of profit which can be made. Moralizing, conservative criticism of this sort would have no effect at all. Criticism must involve formulating one's own goal – emancipation – and must give man the creator a new position vis-à-vis himself and vis-à-vis the world. If the class-struggle prevents this, the theology of labour must not give it a wide berth, but must take it into account and draw conclusions from it which will benefit labour. When political economy was born, the Christians made no attempt to act as midwives. They must make amends for this failure.

Chenu admits that the solution he has put forward could be labelled theological materialism. In so doing he opens the door to a far more dangerous theology – one which would in the last analysis have to be known as a theology of revolution.

Admittedly, Chenu does not go as far as that, or could not do so at that date (1955).

Yet the idea of a divine order made up of connections between man and nature, in which man would create himself and be the creator, has now been voiced, compelling theologians to take their reflections a stage further.

4

But what particularly excites and attracts the theologian who is aware of the incorrigible conservatism of the old theological schemas is just this business of stepping into the future, along a path which is opened up by work and is always being opened up again and again – the secular 'tomorrow' and the place which Christianity will have in it. The future and future history interest him in so far as they are due to receive the honorary title of the Kingdom of God. But what can the Kingdom of God mean, when it is now clear that it cannot possibly be some statically perfect interconnecting *ordo*?

Another leading modern theologian, the Jesuit Karl Rahner, writes that Christianity does not think in terms of a concrete course of history, evolving towards the Kingdom of God by means of its own dynamism.

Each state which we can possibly imagine ourselves attaining in the future, all the brilliant successes which have been scored in conquering the macrocosm, the rich yield of exploitable energy in the microcosm, the way our lives are systematically getting longer, all the wealth of a 'society in profusion', putting a stop to the threat of war for all time, a classless, humanized society – or whatever: we will still always be infinitely far away from the perfection of the Kingdom of God.

Rahner does not, however, wish to put a nihilistic interpretation on the eschatological message. He is in fact interested purely and simply in the fact that, *for the Christian*, the absolute future which men long for so passionately *is already there*, has already occurred: it is there where God and man come together in history, in Christ. From this point of view, though from this point of view alone, everything which will exist in the future has already occurred for the Christian, already been overcome. Thus Christian thought acquires a vast understanding of negation and travels beyond all the horizons that have so far been reached. But this makes it all the more urgent that in the *human* dimension everything still remains to be done in order to achieve the Kingdom of God. Thus the future reveals itself to the Christian's gaze as the realm of man's creative activity, an activity which is always dynamically extending its boundaries further and further – the realm which Pierre Teilhard de Chardin contemplates with such enthusiasm:

We must realize that the continually more complete industrialization of the earth is simply the humano-collective form of a universal process of vitalization which, in this as in all the other cases, can only lead, if we know the right way in which to approach it, to interiorization and to freedom ... The unification of the earth [begins] to convolute upon itself, and so attack the real as one single spearhead.[2]

In his vision men move towards an earth on which their requirements and interests constantly increase, and this will eventually lead to everything being explored, all the ins and outs being examined.

Now that our planet has reached its present level, no physical or psychic force seems capable of preventing man, for millions of years still, from seeking, inventing and creating in every direction ... If biology is extra-polated to its extreme point (and this time ahead of us), it leads us to ... the hypothesis of a universal focus (I have called it Omega), no longer one of physical expansion of exteriorization, but of psychic interiorization.[3]

However fantastic the possibilities open to mankind, and whether or not it seems probable that they will be realized, Rahner does not see them as the 'omega point', the Kingdom of God, the absolute future. Rahner's theology is radical: he refuses to consider each version of the future thought of or planned by man as absolute. This refusal does not just stem from the necessity to construct a defensive position for the *absolutum* of God, but appears to be primarily methodological. This is indeed the only way Rahner can devise an argument for rejecting every attempt made by the Church to stipulate that one specific type of earthly system is obligatory, on the grounds that it is inadequate both from the Christian angle and from the theological angle. He is convinced that the Christian eschatological doctrine cannot be and may not be a social doctrine for life on earth, and that it may not force Christians to accept binding rules concerning their attitude to economic or socio-political questions. He considers that every schema for a social order which makes the ambitious claim that it is a complete, per-fect, absolute prototype for constructing society is Utopian. All that he basically demands of the Christian is that he should be capable of contrasting such a schema with the absolute future – the idea being that this comparison will make him more radical in his readiness to undertake creative action.

The reverse is also true: if looked at in the light of an absolute future, every social order in which man can realize himself 'more', i.e. more totally, seems to Rahner to be an 'order of love'; in its own way it is nearer the Kingdom of God.

If we interpret Rahner's idea about the absolute future as an open *question*, rather than an answer, it is exceptionally fruitful: after all, Marxism, always ready to undertake creative action, asks precisely the same question, with a similar degree of urgency; it acquires particular significance in the areas where one wants to pursue a policy on a really large scale; indeed it is, or can become, a reason for dissociating oneself for good and all from capitalism, and from all the clerical attempts which are merely directed at reforming it, even those which are scarcely perceptible on the surface; but on the other hand, it *can* form the basis of an unbiased attitude to Socialism, and to the efforts made by Communism, which must at any rate be thought of as thoroughly open.

Rahner himself firmly believes that it will be utterly natural for Christians to be grouped into various different socio-political formations *as Christians*, for them to be divided in this respect, indeed even for them to fight among themselves; but this in-fighting cannot end any other way but in the struggle to place a stronger and clearer emphasis on the order of love in a specific social organism.

In view of these utterly new relationships, adherents of this theology begin to ask themselves what being a Christian really means in this complex situation; and how religious faith is still possible in an age which leaves the business of constructing the future totally in the hands of the secular powers, and what its value is in such circumstances.

Religious crisis? Yes, it really does look as if there is one. When the struggle for hyper-civilization stops at nothing, and even the invisible limits of the cosmos are broken down, when we are assailed from all sides by a large number of ideologists, a motley crew of philosophical and artistic currents, then it really can look as if Christianity were no longer capable of holding its own among so many rivals; especially in those areas where it merely sticks timidly and narrow-mindedly to its old stereotyped ideas and attitudes. But Rahner is convinced that the fear which causes this state of affairs is clerical and conservative. For, he asks, what does Christianity impart to us in point of fact? God? Other religions do that too. That is precisely why Rahner does not set too much store by ontological proofs of God's existence. He makes no attempt whatsoever to preach them. Instead, he stands by Pascal's 'wager argument': to place a bet on God's existence, in the absence of any striking evidence to the contrary, is both logical and fruitful as far as this life is concerned. In this new theology God does not appear as an object, but as the tension between 'outside us' and 'within us': he represents transcendence, and is infinitely mysterious. *Man* is constantly attempting to decipher him, using his self-conscious activity and devoting his efforts to objects, but without ever getting any peace. Man feels himself to be 'an indefinability which has come to its senses'; he expresses himself as an infinite question. God is therefore the infinite, absolute answer to this question.

In Rahner's view, Christianity's superiority over all other religions results quite simply from the fact that this secret was spoken of, but this did not stop it being a secret – in that God and man meet in the Godman, in Christ. This meant that man's secret became historically tangible; he eventually made it aware of itself, and from then on it was transformed into the hidden driving force motivating the whole of his creative activity in history.

We cannot dispute the loftiness of Rahner's thinking: yes, it all fits in, the original version of Christianity formulated in the time of Jesus does involve this hoministic challenge.

Admittedly, another thing that fits in is that in the course of time the intervention of theology has so distorted this challenge that it has become illegible. What we have here is a palimpsest: it is only on the underneath layer that we can find the text, which was written not by God, but by a man. We revere him across all the ups and downs of the centuries, whoever he may have been. The new anthropological attitude of theology helps Rahner not only to overcome the clerical fear in the face of a crisis, but also leads him towards a form of Christianity which is so *immense* that a reflected and purified belief in Jesus Christ forms only a small part of it, though admittedly this may be the most important part.

When people declare that we are living in a time of religious crisis, Rahner sees this observation as totally superficial. To be sure, the Christian is surrounded by a whole host of attitudes and outlooks which are alien and indifferent to Christianity, or even positively hostile to it. If he looks about him, he sees thousands of people, whole cultures, whole periods in history, which are positively non-Christian. He knows that a time will come when Christianity will no longer exist as a matter of course in Europe and in the world.

But in his opinion this situation cannot rock the Christian faith to its foundations, provided that it does not itself succumb to the exhaustion and despair which are washed up along with every grey wave of day-to-day existence.

Even the obstacle which the Church itself puts in the path of belief cannot shake it. Rahner objects to the sort of apologetic Christianity which sees the Church as representing a taboo. The Church is as sinful as it is holy; it is on trial; it is a human institution. The charge preferred against it applies to every single Christian, from the layman right up to the leader of the Church. Being a believer in this day and age means *taking a chance* with the sinful Church. The believer is helped in this by his awareness that Christ is the secret testimony which has been pronounced on us. It is this awareness which rouses him to perform actions enabling man to surpass himself, without thinking of the philistine comforts of eternal salvation, but rather in order to develop an order based on love, and to hear the call of the absolute future. That, according to Rahner, is what makes Christianity eternal and immortal, and allows it to exist in a huge number of different forms. Christianity is to be found, anonymous but nevertheless present, wherever people are facing fearlessly up to life, trying to excel themselves by their actions, and seeking an answer to the secret of their own existence. Even if a man is a primitive positivist, even if he has gone astray in trying to create technical or scientific Utopias, even if he has professed other gods, or no god at all, he can still be one of those who are on the right path, who are coming close to God without realizing it themselves; he can be an 'implicit' Christian. Whenever he appreciates the fact that every creative act in history owed its existence to love and hope, he is being an implicit Christian. For Rahner, no man can fail to be in some way a Christian. The man of longing, the man of never-ending love . . .

His glimmer of light may be tiny, yet . . . Anyone who sets out in this manner may be far from the officially constituted Christianity; he may feel like an atheist, he may think fearfully that he does not believe in God – Christian teaching and conduct of life may appear strange and almost oppressive to him. But he should go on and follow the light shining in the innermost depth of his heart . . . The Christian is not afraid that he will not arrive.[4]

The theory of anonymous Christianity is the most important

practical idea to be put forward by open theology, open Catholicism. It does not merely contain a constructive acceptance of the fact that a large number of religions and attitudes to life can exist side by side, but also establishes an open connection to the various social patterns, irrespective of their concrete (hypothetical or political) relationship to Christianity. Even if this relationship is clearly hostile, this still does not mean, according to open Catholicism, that the system is essentially non-Christian. The Christians' task involves recognizing their true worth, and attempting to induce them to participate in a dialogue with their own reflected form. This applies particularly to the other non-Christian religions, especially those which are older than Christianity. Even if one can point to their various distortions and errors, Rahner is all the same convinced that they contain various nuances which prove that they are legitimate religions.

But according to Rahner, Christians should not behave in a censorious or scornful manner towards declared atheists. He firmly believes that it is only conservative-thinking people who think that atheism stems from malevolence. It would be much better to ask how far Christianity is to blame for atheism, how far it has distorted or misrepresented the original 'Word of God', so that men have eventually turned away from it altogether. Open Christianity is quite simply determined to say 'yes' to everything in the various attitudes, movements and schemas – however far removed from official Christianity – that increases the prospects of love; for love is the *ens primum*, the archetype, in the cosmos of human connections, an uncommonly high stake – high because it is unconditional – placed by the ego for the benefit of one's fellow-men; for this stake alone is capable of fashioning the history of man, which is reproducible in the cosmos, acting as if it were an act of God.

5

Nothing would be easier than to reject the idea of an absolute future and an anonymous Christianity, simply because it is put forward by theologians. We feel that that would be a pity: in so doing we would be destroying the possibility of holding an open dialogue, which is what the situation offers; we would be sealing off one of the important ways of creating a practical policy.

We do certainly have doubts as to whether the idea of an anonymous Christianity will be acceptable to the orthodox 'integralists' within the Catholic Church, at any rate in its present form as 'Christianity without limits'. All of us have great respect for the radical way in which the problems are presented to us, and for the high personal standards which are formulated here; in spite of this we must voice the sceptical question of whether political reality is not being made too abstract, especially since it must be said that not even the most open forms of theology are completely free from certain prejudices in their attitude to Communism; we must also ask whether an interpretation which is so broad-minded is not, in certain circumstances, in danger of being neutral in the very places where indifference or opportunism are inappropriate for everybody, even for the Christian. Such a danger does indeed seem to exist. The men who are known as 'left-wing Catholics' (A. M. Knoll, E. K. Winter, F. Heer, W. Daim) are intellectually closely related to open Catholicism (especially to its critical attitude to the authority of the Church); but both in their own field – theology – and in their interpretation of Communism, they are not very thorough, and they finally arrive at the neutral idea of co-existence, an idea which is as unacceptable to genuine Catholics as it is to genuine Communists. According to their way of looking at it, the Christian would have to remain neutral in his attitude to the antagonism between socialism and capitalism; and the Communist would have to do the same when faced with the antagonism between theism and atheism. But it is quite clear that no one would be able to find a way out of this confused situation.

And another thing: a Communist will not accept the honorary title of 'anonymous Christian'. Not because the whole idea sets his teeth on edge. Nor out of political narrow-mindedness. The motives underlying his rejection are more serious.

Despite all the fundamental ideological and philosophical reservations, despite the questions which Marxists will feel to be unclear and not properly thought out, despite all the doubts which they must voice as political thinkers, despite all these factors, this change in theological thinking is so important that we cannot pass it over lightly. Indeed it was not restricted to abstract theoretical reflections. The spirit of open Catholicism was even admitted into the halls at St Peter's where the Ecumenical Council of the Churches was assembled for its three-year session. It attempted to insinuate itself into the Council's discussions. This attempt was not totally abortive, though it did not score a really sensational success.

But open Catholicism has yet another much greater significance for Marxists. The questions raised by the new theology affect the very foundations of their outlook on life. Of every outlook on life. The merit of the theologians who postulate an absolute future lies in the radical way they are asking these questions today: there is no way of dodging them.

It is not as if they were questions which the Marxists knew nothing about, or had no feeling for. They have been asking them right from the outset, the most notable among them being Marx, Engels, Lenin, Gramsci and a whole lot of others; though of course they asked them in a different context, and within a philosophical framework which was much more highly organized than that of open Catholicism. So Marxism scores a plus here, but it also scores a minus. These questions might indeed be overlooked in certain circumstances, or pushed to one side. This has happened at certain points, during the development of Marxism, which is not, however, a type of Positivism, nor a type of Scientism, nor a type of Rationalism. Its shrewdest critics are aware of this, or at any rate sense it. That is why it appeals to them.

Footnotes

1) M. D. Chenu: *Work and the Divine Cosmos*, 1956.

2) Pierre Teilhard de Chardin: *Man's Place in Nature*, translated by René Hague, Collins, Fontana, 1971, pp. 105, 107.

3) ibid. pp. 112, 116.

4) Karl Rahner: *Theological Investigations*, V, trans. Karl H. Kruger, Darton, Longman & Todd, 1966, p. 21.

4
APPEAL

... it was the work of man, all over the place, full of blood and enthusiasm, full of naïve faith and a far-reaching knowledge of the essential
facts of the situation, full of cruelty and a love rich in imagination; it
contained filth, hunger, lice, desertion, treason, a simple and trans-
parently clear purity of action, a surfeit of pleasures, a bird's wing, a
return to the age of fire-arms, the constant expectation of a bullet fired
in hatred – a résumé of all the many contrasts life has to offer, but with
the best outstripping the worst, extremes, border-line situations, birth
accompanied by labour pains ...

The great October Revolution – for that is what this pen-portrait
jotted down somewhere or other by Isaac Babel refers to – was not
'holy'. It did not need any mysticism, any saints with their legends,
any theology, to remain a living memory for succeeding generations,
a vast image which can never be wiped out by wishful thinking.

Right down in the depths where subjective motivations lie hidden,
the class waging the revolution used it to lay claim to the absolute
future of *man*, a future in which he would be able to develop all his
various attributes to the full.

Although the socialist revolution may have run a tumultuous and
zig-zag course, evidence of this claim can be seen in the impatient
anticipation and codification of its illusions. And although the
future may be even more complicated than the past, it never lost
this basic dimension, and will never lose it, unless it throws in the
sponge itself.

Yet the socialist revolution was not a universal hominstic challenge 'to everyone'. It was, is and will be a practical act, a conscious
intrusion by the working class into the tapestry of history, their

attack being launched from the new positions which they were occupying for the first time ever. An onlooker may well find that the clarity of the original challenge is eclipsed or lost in the bewildering tangle of changes. And in certain cases even those who are at the heart of the struggle may be hard put to hear it. But for those who owe their existence to the actions performed by the revolution, who are aware of this and are full of sympathy for it, its challenge is permanently alive and topical.

Over and above this 'confession', the title 'anonymous Christian' is totally unacceptable to the Communist. The 'absolute future' really represents a claim which is constantly being renewed, an incessant challenge to man as a conscious living being. It demands an absolute, sovereign answer; for without this he would be incapable of achieving anything of any *productive* value. He would simply be able to reproduce himself as an intelligent animal, but that would be all. And yet this challenge does not only come up against the fact that individuals are not sovereign, against their historical limitations, the narrow-mindedness of their opinions – which are full of errors – and their actions; it also comes up against an element of non-sovereignty in their existence, i.e. against the fact of death. There is a contradiction here, comments Engels, as he discusses the question in his arguments with Dühring.

A present-day Marxist can only be extremely surprised at the carelessly positivistic way people read the lines where Engels says that this contradiction cannot be solved, unless we are allowed to presuppose an infinite progression in an infinite, or at least for us practically infinite, succession of human races. What else is Engels saying here, but that the absolute claim – this reality which is so deeply rooted in man, which is always being uttered anew and is always becoming necessary to society all over again – must remain unanswered on principle? Nowhere in his writings does Engels assume that mankind will survive for an infinite length of time, and he makes no mention whatsoever of guaranteeing it; he even admits elsewhere that the opposite is possible. The absolute postulates made by man form a systematic sequence of questions, but they do not provide any answers. If we concede this, all that is left is the question of what man is exposing himself to as a result. To a vacuum perhaps? To nothingness? Yes, provided that we stick to this system of asking questions.

But in order to formulate this claim *in a new way*, the Communist must pass through the sphere of activity, must know how to put up with having this activity slandered, with being threatened by nothingness, with disappointment.

His existential position is more easily undermined than that of the Christian. It does not allow him to counterbalance the absolute question with the absolute answer. If it did, he would lose that very thing for which his challenge qualifies him: the ability to surpass himself by his actions.

That is why he cannot accept the honorary title 'anonymous Christian'. This would be too cheap a method of shaking off his misery, his hopelessness and his claims. If he were a Christian – even an anonymous one – he would be less than he is capable of being.

2

The aspect which belongs exclusively to Communism is the epoch-making act of emancipation. It is an act which troubles the spirit, rather than one motivated by spiritless pragmatism.

The result is that it is more difficult to be a Communist than to be a Christian. For the Communist exposes himself to a danger of which the Christian is totally unaware: the danger that he may disappoint many people in their hopes and expectations of achieving a Utopia. They are right to cherish such hopes, but they will not be fulfilled in their lifetime. That is why Socialism has its traitors, its renegades, its one-time friends who are now its enemies; it also has luke-warm supporters. It carries its dead along with it, plus the people it has put to death. Its strength lies in the courage with which it recognizes its own weakness, with which it is prepared to submit it to the verdict of history.

And yet it will never leave its post.

Why?

Yes, why, indeed?

Part III

ATHEISM TAKES A
LOOK AT ITSELF

ATHEISM WITHIN SOCIALISM

1

The moment when one takes a close look at oneself is a time for standing still, a time for productive tranquillity. Our sense of responsibility leads us to make an attempt to reflect on the new meanings in those elements which are inalienable, which we cannot give up without giving ourselves up as well. We endeavour to reassemble everything we have done so far, including the methods we used and the factors which induced us to act in that way. We try to incorporate whole complexes of well-known ideas and past actions into those deeper strata in which reality comes to light today. If they do not fit in with these strata, we want to establish why this is so. We want to understand the reason, we want to understand *ourselves*.

This, I feel, is where reflecting quietly on oneself differs from radical criticism of everything which has gone before, and also from a panicky apology for one's past deeds. Radical criticism involves unearthing shortcomings and deformities, exposing 'inexplicable oversights' and carping in a thoroughly petty fashion at serious matters, exercising one's polished wit at their expense; but in so doing, such critics demonstrate their failure to understand the fact that nothing in history can be kept secret, thus putting themselves on a par with more conservative people attempting to justify themselves. But if we think hard about this question, these two extreme attitudes will give way to a matter-of-factness which is not afraid of the past; in fact it is not unduly concerned with the past at all, because we know that we must find ways of stepping beyond the present into tomorrow.

Oh, yes, in examining ourselves our first priority is to understand ourselves from the historical angle. That is the only way we will be able to succeed in looking beyond our own house, as we emerge from the tranquil concentration of the night into the early morning and all the conflicts of everyday existence.

2

In the early days of Socialism in Czechoslovakia, atheism stemmed from the need to fight against the reaction started by the clergy; this reactionary attitude had the upper hand both in the political parties which had been in existence before February 1948 and in the ecclesiastical hierarchy, particularly among the higher Church dignitaries. Yet there was plenty of goodwill about. After the February Revolution, the first President remained faithful to an old tradition by stepping straight from the polling ceremony into St Vitus's Cathedral to attend the *Te Deum* presided over by the Archbishop of Prague. Many Communists and atheists blamed him for this at the time. But the Communist Party was determined to put into practice its scheme for a dictatorship by the proletariat on a wider basis, in the form of a collaboration between all the various progressive forces in the population. Its first constitution had tabulated this resolution.

Another source for the atheism of that period was the Communists' conviction – or at any rate this applies particularly to them – that a socialist system set up on a scientific basis had no need of religion; that in so far as religion is still in existence and will continue to exist, it is more of a brake on politics and ideology, acting as a damper on one's creative energies and as a subversive factor demoralizing the enthusiasm which is necessary for setting up a new system. They were quite right at the time: not only was official Christianity not favourably disposed towards Socialism, its whole social doctrine and its political commitments were overtly anti-Communist.

During the brief period when the original political blueprint of the Communist Party was being distorted, atheism came to a head, because in practical political work the fundamental political criterion underlying the Marxist concept of atheism temporarily disappeared from view: i.e. the stipulation that one should not equate believers with the Church, nor religious conviction with the political body of the clergy. A frontal attack was launched against religion, from the standpoint of administration, politics and ideology; this was part of a broadly based political 'theory' concerning the need to aggravate the class war. This was the period in which certain atheist stereotypes were being formulated, and it also saw the introduction of certain practices which remained in fashion for varying lengths of time, even after the Communist Party had expressly dissociated itself from them in the middle of the fifties.

The atheistic conviction which formed the framework of this period was an extremely rigorous one. It was based on the view that the seizure of power by the working class and the construction of a socialist society ought to have wiped out any trace of the social and class-ridden roots of religion. If any trace of religion had survived, this was a mere remnant in the consciousness of the bourgeoisie, which was being strengthened by the activities of the Churches and was frequently being misused by them in their fight against Socialism. This resulted in what appears to be a perfectly logical line of reasoning, which says that every believer is for that reason alone a potential opponent of Communism. That was why people working in what are known as 'executive posts' were requested to withdraw from the Church in order to prove that they had a positive attitude to the constitution of the people's democracy; that is also why every confidential report contained a stereotyped question asking whether the employee had come properly to terms with the religious question.

It was felt that the idealistic influence of religion was to be curtailed as far as possible, regardless of whether it was linked to any one denomination, or whether it was merely a matter of traces of religion in customs or cultural traditions, in literature or in art. Old legends and tales were revamped to rid them of any religious motifs they might contain; old customs bound up with the Christian tradition were replaced by new ones, while any works of art and cultural values dating from the classical world which could not be touched up so as to fit with atheist thinking were simply wiped out of the public consciousness.

The reader will understand that it is not our intention to vent our irony on this practice – as sometimes happens – or to sit in judgement after the event, as it were; what we want to do is far more important – i.e. we want to understand the motives underlying this behaviour: it seemed as if such methods would succeed in creating a religious vacuum in which religion would quietly fade away, disappearing from the human consciousness of its own accord and collapsing completely as soon as the older generation had died out.

The old defunct ideas were to be replaced by science: that is, by positive scientific attitudes and the formation of a general socialist conscience. Atheistic propaganda went to great lengths to prove that religious faith conflicted with scientific findings in every possible way, and that to continue, in this new scientific age, to believe in the fictions dreamed up by religion was to adopt an obscurantist attitude which was quite indefensible. The contrast between belief and scientific reason was carried to extremes.

So atheists in that period were acting out of expressly political and pedagogic motives: they wanted to take in hand those people who were not yet ready to tear themselves away from the influence of the Church, and were still slaves to religious theories which had long ago been discarded, so that they could influence them in accordance with the spirit of socialist progress. They felt that pressure must be brought to bear wherever people were adhering too long or too obstinately to such theories. They had their eye on the future, and thought that it had already drawn near – that future in which we would finally arrive at the ideal social structure of Socialism, in which there would be no traces of the social systems which flourished by exploiting the workers, in which there would be no more religious communities to support, where cathedrals would be transformed into museums wherever possible, or perhaps into concert-halls, where God would at last be dead. This prospect had many elements likely to satisfy the atheist: first and foremost because the theoretical demands of Marxism seemed to be fulfilled in such a society, for Marxism does not in fact reckon on the continued existence of God; secondly because the social pattern within socialism was no longer beset by a tricky factor which can give rise to political complications; and also because he was witnessing the frustration of that obscurantist and humiliating ideology which makes it so exceedingly difficult to exert a standardized ideological influence. This vision possessed considerable appeal. The atheist felt that a world without God would be clearer and easier to control, in both the political and social spheres.

Admittedly, he knew from experience that there was still a long way to go before the present situation began to resemble the ideal situation. But he believed that politics could bridge the gap. He was familiar with the general political principles formulated by Leninism as an answer to the religious question. He noted the decisions reached by the Party for straightening out such aberrations. But he did not see why, in the interests of a goal of which he was convinced, he should not implement the same policy in all the various fields where this was possible, treating it as an instrument for speeding up the whole process.

The atheist had no doubts about himself. In so far as he still mentally associated religion in general with himself, he was delighted not to be mixed up in the confusion of religion. He felt free. Being able to enjoy the reality of socialism without hindrance, joining enthusiastically in the business of setting up a socialist state, delighting in success, feeling certain about the prospects for the future, and convinced that the basic problems had been solved – all these factors led him to make a thoroughly tendentious examination of each and every question from the political angle; and the combined effect of all this was too powerful for him to need to fritter away his time in useless discussions. The type of atheism which resulted from this first-hand delight in freedom and socialism represented a sort of social experience; it had a strong emotional appeal and was the driving force behind social and political action. Being totally wrapped up in himself, the atheist wished the whole of society and every individual citizen to attain an equal degree of self-awareness. It was even a militant atheism – at least this is true of the type of atheism which was most characteristic of this particular period.

We must now make it clear that this type of optimistic atheism – totally committed, inflexible, pedagogic – belongs irretrievably to the past; but is there any reason to regret this? Or should we perhaps agree with those arrogant, mocking and nihilistic critics who sometimes consider not just this type of atheism, but atheism in general to be a thoroughly antiquated idea?

It seems to us a matter of urgency that we should acquaint ourselves with the ideas and motives of that type of atheism, and reconstruct the thought-pattern which allowed such motives to become so virulent.

3

The remarkable thing about this type of atheism, which developed historically, is that its greatest and most immediately effective strength lies in its illusions, in its simplifications and in its errors.

It is closely bound up with the early years of socialism and the first stages of its construction. It overestimates the importance of these years for the disappearance of religion. It often mistakes this process for a solitary occurrence, and also tends erroneously to think of the long-drawn-out and complicated struggle as a decree which occurred before the event. Ideal and abstract goals which are the main motivation behind all activity are projected forward into the imperfect factual world which is constantly evolving. Ideological uniformity, which can only be reached gradually, as one standardized element among a multiplicity of elements, is to be brought about as rapidly as possible; and this is to be done in such a way that it penetrates every layer of society. Even when it is obvious from the outset that this is a long-term requirement, in practice atheists develop it into a policy calculated on a short-term basis. Since a watched pot never boils, the campaigns had to be repeated over and over again. The atheists clearly failed to understand that forming a whole philosophy of life is a process which evolves according to its own inherent laws and proceeds relatively independently, admitting of no outside interference.

In their attack against religious belief, against its vague ecstatic emotionalism, the atheists turned to rationalism for help. This furnished atheism with those elements which are the prerogative of rationalism: positive scientific views taken from astronomy, physics, chemistry and biology. This scientific view of life, composed

154

as it is of a number of separate fragments of information, does, it is true, contain a series of counter-arguments against the view put forward by 'natural theology', which sees God as the 'Great Watchmaker' of the universe. But those who accept this theory do not ask either the people whom it is supposed to influence, or themselves, what exactly the point is of having an idea or image of God, if this cannot be defended from the point of view of scientific causality. The scientific arguments put forward by atheists usually finish up with the observation that religion is a preposterous and totally irrational business; but in saying this they do not even reach the stage where the real problems begin for science. Their lack of intelligence can be seen in the fact that they cannot imagine religion as anything but anthropomorphic, and are utterly helpless when faced with various diverging religious theories; above all, they do not know what to make of religious experiences, because these lie outside their powers of comprehension. Atheists of this type are quite unable to answer the frequent question as to how a highly educated scientist who is actively engaged on scientific research can possibly possess an equally profound and active belief in God.

But if scientifically motivated atheists do not at least ask themselves whether their way of studying the world can also acquire some sort of *human* meaning, they are thoroughly lacking in intelligence and do not equal the intellectual level of Christianity, still less that of Marxism. This type of atheist retains his self-confidence as long as he has the feeling that he can rely on opinions which are absolutely safe, exact and irrefutable. He begins to waver as soon as he notices – as he must – that he and his arguments are not being given a hearing.

The type of atheism we are discussing here was constitutionally anti-theistic. The atheist was haunted by the idea that so many people had an image of God firmly implanted within their brains. He rightly connected the fustiness of a religious life, which he could still remember from his childhood, the pious attitude which had always been distasteful to him and which he could still see when he looked about him, with the primitive nature of religious theories which are not worthy of man. He thought it his duty to refute this puerile self-deception. This was a reversed kind of tropism; the atheist turned his gaze in the direction from which he could feel the *darkness* coming towards him. But the fight against the religious obscurantism which really does exist, no question about it, against the baser, uncultured, bottom-of-the-barrel forms of Christian or religious belief, against every kind of superstition and fanaticism, is not entirely warranted and does come up against certain limits. If this fact is not recognized, anti-theism becomes the unintentional ally of political clericalism: it tips off the clergy about what has been discredited and the traditions it must break with.

The hatred of God which is the underlying motive of anti-theism is an important element in any convinced belief; virtually everybody with a genuine religious conviction has been consumed by a rebellious anti-theism at least once.

The illusions, simplifications and errors prevalent in this type of atheism would scarcely be as sure of themselves and as tenacious, if they had not also found theoretical support in the doctrines and way of thinking formulated by Stalinism, after it had cut down dialectical materialism to a mechanistic materialism of the type which had been current before Marx came on the scene. This is clearly the origin of the new absolute outlook of science, which encouraged the emergence of a new, very vulgar form of speculative natural philosophy; uncritical confidence in what is known as 'common sense', and in the possibility of manipulating one's fellow-men, is also rooted in this. Marx's materialistic view of history was divided up for the 'short course' into a series of unconnected themes, and was thus transformed into the academic discipline known as 'historical materialism'. Its theses on the relationship between substructure and superstructure, which were in due course being discussed according to the methods of Scholasticism, were applied to the field of religion, but here they were not suitable for use as an analytical tool.

In so far as historical materialism took the place of the content which had formerly been supplied by specific forms of sociology, the theoretical substructure was not broad enough for atheism. Its claim to be known as a 'scientific atheism' did not come true.

4

Does this mean that all this work, to which many years had been sacrificed, was wasted, superfluous, wrong? No, certainly not. It was even to a large extent politically necessary, and it fulfilled the task it had been set wherever the clergy was anxious to pursue an anti-socialistic policy. It was quite in order in the struggle against the most obscure, most primitive and most fanatical forms and manifestations of religious belief. The problem which it now comes up against lies elsewhere: we must point out how complicated the factors underlying even this primarily pedagogic-cum-political form of atheism were. If we understand this we will not cherish the illusion that being an atheist is a matter of course; that this attitude is a logical product of the Marxist outlook on life, being just one part of the whole.

In point of fact the opposite is true: Marxism is essentially atheistic. Or to put it another way: it is atheism which provides the radical aspect of the Marxist philosophy of life. Without it, both Marx's plan for a 'total man' and his concept of Communism are equally inconceivable.

That is why Marxist atheism cannot exist by itself as a spontaneous attitude; nor can it be theoretically nurtured as if it were some sort of fringe branch of science, as a 'scientific atheism' which is only very loosely connected with the 'principal problems of philosophy and sociology'.

Marxist atheism is a point of view reached after careful reflection. It goes beyond religion, for it includes all the different historical phases in the development and criticism of Christianity and takes them over.

It is on its travels – with all the hardships involved in any long journey.

2

THE EMANCIPATION
OF ATHEISM

1

'God is dead!'

The news has been going the rounds ever since the Renaissance; at first it was a secret, passed on in whispers, but later it became louder and louder and increasingly self-confident.

'Long live God!' that is the echo which has been ringing out persistently down to the present day.

Marxists must listen carefully to the content of both these reports.

2

Atheism reached its first high-point in the modern era in the Enlightenment which took place in eighteenth-century France.

In the writings of the Enlightenment philosophers reason knocked God and the King off their thrones and condemned them resolutely to the guillotine; then it ripped off their golden robes and set a dunce's cap on their heads; but in so doing it achieved no more than the bourgeoisie were to do a decade or two later in their revolution, except that their action was practical rather than theoretical.

The outcome was bourgeois atheism; it sees *God* as complementing the *animal* monarchy which was already in existence; what an animal our beloved king is, after all! This alliance resulted in the birth of the power of irrationality; this now took over the reins of power, and the impotence and sickness of reason testifies to this.

The bulky tomes of the Enlightenment philosophers, from La Mettrie to Holback, Diderot to Helvetius, Voltaire to Rousseau, tried to diagnose this state of affairs in their critical sections. These attempts always finished with the same recipe for salvation: both monarchs must be put to death as soon as possible. Reason is to take their place on the throne. The Enlightenment writers expect her to be able to contract a decent marriage with nature; for although so far they have been compelled to live in sin, their union has already borne rich fruit. The Enlightenment philosophers drew up an inventory of these fruits in their *Encyclopédie, ou Dictionnaire Raisonné des Sciences, des Arts et des Métiers*. They were convinced that this marriage would free man from the chains of religion for ever. This meant that the objective world would no longer be able to escape into areas where reason could not follow, and where the theologians were in control. Everything would become visible, everything would be relinquished.

They believed that reason would grant universal freedom. By being 'extroverted', turning their attention totally outwards, they would at last catch a glimpse of the Great Mother as she really is, physically enticing, subject to her own passion, which is the basis of her strength. That is why the bourgeois Enlightenment attaches such importance to science and technical skills: they are the tools of *possession*. The only things which are acceptable to reason are things which man can possess, i.e. which he can acquire for himself as objects and which he can negotiate with at will – even if he must do so within a framework of unalterable natural laws. Reason is suspicious of anything which, for one reason or another, refuses to be possessed: she senses in such things a feeling of irrationality, of the old province of the theologians. Anything which cannot be properly calculated is intolerable to reason, because that means it cannot be rationalized either. She therefore callously excludes from her realm everything which is non-conformist, for she cannot *count on* it. Reason as conceived by the Enlightenment is always close to terror. So what she thinks of as a reasonable social order is one where she can compare the most widely varied phenomena according to the primitive, democratic principle of counting them off – that principle which is the essential prerequisite for technology and for manipulating objects. This means that things and people appear as objective units which are moved from place to place according to rational rules, their progress being strictly disciplined. The rationality of this system is proved by its effectiveness, by the returns, profit and capital which it yields. Knowledge is power.

The realm of reason devised by the Enlightenment philosophers was an ideal version of the realm of the bourgeoisie; Engels's value judgement really does hit the nail on the head. Reason's hatred of the irrationality of religion stemmed from totally practical interests. That is why her atheism was not total, why it was not a value which makes men stand out as men. It was a special standpoint which can be accounted for by the bourgeoisie's claim to power. It was more operational than heart-felt. It stood for something else, not for itself.

Admittedly, there are also a number of positive aspects in this enlightened atheism subscribed to by the bourgeoisie, and these form a stable element in modern thinking, and thence *an essential factor* in Marxist atheism. The elements we welcome in the Enlightenment are always to be found in Marxist atheism in those areas where our struggle for a rational settlement of the whole affair (in which the quantitative point of view cannot be glossed over) clashes with the mythical contemplation of the objective world; wherever, in our militant set-to with politico-clerical Christianity, we consciously accept atheism as a particular standpoint with overtones of the class conflict.

This must be said if we are to be able to make a categorical rejection of the business of making these elements absolute – which is so characteristic of the atheism of the Enlightenment. For this idea must be rejected, because it has far-reaching consequences. The Enlightenment equated reason with power. Everything which is contrary to reason can be ruled out if only we use the methods of reason properly. In this the Enlightenment philosophers even succeeded in mystifying themselves. They considered that reason dominates history and can therefore eliminate history at will. They were so absorbed by the vision of universal *possession* that they did not notice that reason did not only draw up and impose rules, but also had rules imposed on her. They did not admit to themselves that, just as reason takes possession of things and manipulates them, so she is herself overwhelmed and manipulated by them; she is subject as well as sovereign.

That is why the Enlightenment thinkers had the misfortune to see their fruitful theory of rationalization turning *in practice* into brutality, violence, aggression and even into a counterthrust from the forces of irrationality. The reason of the Enlightenment 'inevitably generated irrationality' (Kosík).[1]

Even before the bourgeoisie, in their cynical attempt to debase all values by thinking of them in terms of goods, property and capital, had confirmed this inevitable process, the Enlightenment gave advance confirmation itself. The Marquis de Sade is also part of the Enlightenment. In his philosophy of cruelty, de Sade paints an expressive picture of everything that lies hidden behind the veiled countenance of enlightened reason. His atheism does not only lead in the end to the execution of God, and to the idealization of an auspicious rule of reason; it also betrays a certain amount of what is to be found lurking behind the scenes, in the cosy realm of the day-to-day reign of reason, and well camouflaged by a general agreement on moral standards of upright behaviour. If everything is an object, manipulation represents the height of power and becomes a matter of course; the more callous, brutal and aggressive such manipulation is, the closer it comes to fulfilling its mission. It offers orgiastic enjoyment of a pleasure which stems from power and despotic authority.

De Sade's philosophy is the voice of cynical reason, twisting her virtuous features into a distorted grimace because she already has a foreboding of what is going to happen to her.

The reason of the Enlightenment announces the death of God. In so doing, she opens up some important paths along which man can pursue the course of progress. But she does not take seriously the subject which extricates itself from her clutches, escaping beyond the limits of mere possession; and so she resorts to violence and thus destroys at a single stroke her own much-vaunted propriety. Her throne is eaten away by irrationality, because she has not succeeded in keeping it under control.

3

God is dead! That was the cry which rang out at the end of the eighteenth century, in Germany as well as France. But how different the situation was there! In France, the philosophers of the Enlightenment dealt a crushing blow to religion. After the storm had subsided, the bourgeoisie became a level-headed force which didn't take its atheism or its enlightened ideas too seriously.

The atheism of the German bourgeoisie, following in the footsteps of Marx, had its roots in Luther's Reformation. The thoroughly wretched situation in Germany had the effect of compelling the Germans to transform their actual interests into philosophical-cum-religious interests, if they wanted to become aware of them at all. That is why the brand of atheism which declares that religion is absolutely nonsensical is the exception in Germany, rather than the rule. As far as the Germans were concerned, and this applies even to the German adherents of the Enlightenment, religion always has some sort of meaning: they see it as reflecting the conflicts they have staged in history. Admittedly, this is a disadvantage. It means that events are not understood as they really are, unvarnished, but as manifestations of changes in history and in religion. The importance of religion is extraordinarily overrated in Germany; this blunts the social criticism made by atheism, i.e. atheism as a political standpoint specifically directed against feudalism. But this disadvantage is offset by the fact that there is less of a tendency to make atheism absolute by seeing it as a mere expedient in the political struggle for power, and its more general significance is therefore thrown into relief.

The breath of freedom which wafted over the Rhine into Germany encountered such a fusty atmosphere that revolutionary action was absolutely out of the question: instead, it was transformed into a philosophizing spirit, in the person of Hegel. In those of his works written during his theological period, freedom appears as a challenge which runs counter to everything introduced to the consciousness as a revealed truth, as a *positivum*. Christianity in particular is just such a positive, absolute religion. Hegel discovered that the historical basis of Christianity's uncritical position lay in the conflict between the spirit of classical antiquity and that of Judaism. Unlike the classical world, the Jews were aware that the finite and the infinite, life and death, individuality and society are at odds with each other. The aim of Jesus's doctrine is to heal this breach. But he is dragged to the place of execution and dies without reaching his goal. It has become evident that his kingdom is not of this world. So Christianity strengthens the breach between subject and object. It divides men up into this world and the next world, body and soul, life and death, the finite and the infinite. But for Hegel, this religious alienation contains some very real problems: the individual is absorbed by 'the other world', i.e. by society, by the universe of inter-relationships; the body stands in the way of the high-flying ambitions of the spirit when it wishes to soar upwards; in death all life is extinguished; everything which is finite falls headlong into the abyss of infinity; despair is a millstone round the neck of happiness. Christianity makes these facts absolute: it makes human consciousness an *unhappy consciousness*. *That is why* it is compelled to hold its own as a positive religion.

So Hegel does not think of religion as absurd. The substance which Christianity gives to religion does not seem to him to be so obscure as not to be even worth bothering about. Rather the reverse: he feels that it offers a historically justified attempt to find a solution to a *general* problem, which *must* be played out to the end so that we can fully appreciate how ineffective it is.

In criticizing Christianity, he is therefore also criticizing the positivism of the classical world. In spite of the lucid and clearly articulated *unity* of its cosmos, the Greek *polis* was unable to prevent man becoming aware of his unhappiness; on the other hand, Christianity did not permit man in his divided state to become aware of his happiness. But man is both at the mercy of unhappiness and in control of his happiness. A high-level synthesis is needed to preserve and eliminate these two factors simultaneously: i.e. what is needed is the work of the consciousness as it progresses towards emancipation. Man must pass beyond the limits of unhappiness, so that he can seize hold of the happiness which resides in the sort of freedom which is worthy of him. This is no idle phrase as far as Hegel is concerned.

We notice that Hegel has a deep-seated understanding of the seriousness and onerousness of life. He rejects the carefree optimism which asserts that in the last analysis everything is 'do-able' if only we have the appropriate means at our disposal. He feels that the happy-go-lucky spirit of antiquity, proficient in all possible skills, is the embodiment of this type of optimism. The other pole of existence, unhappiness, broods over it like a cloud of fate raining down thunderbolts which man cannot escape. Life consisted of enjoying oneself, until death and the gloom of Hades came along. Life was possessing things. Man was a mere being: happy unconsciousness.

Christianity eliminates this state of happy unconsciousness by reflecting on it. It has a deep-seated understanding of everything which arises as three-dimensional time flows by, of everything which withers away in the temporal world and sinks into infinity. It takes the difficult moments into account and is familiar with the ultimate experience – death. Yet Christianity sees this burdensome existence as absolute: it would like to be able to overcome it, but is incapable of doing so. It pays for this in the end by revaluing *nothingness* until it is worth *everything*. Just as the classical world is light-hearted, so Christianity is heavy-hearted; it is an unhappy consciousness.

Hegel concludes his study of these two stages in the evolution of consciousness – which cancel each other out – as follows:

We see that this 'unhappy consciousness' constitutes the counterpart and the complement of the perfectly happy consciousness, that of comedy ... it means, in other words, the complete relinquishment and emptying of substance. The former, on the contrary, is conversely the tragic fate that befalls certainty of self which aims at being absolute, at being self-sufficient. It is consciousness of the loss of everything of significance in this certainty of itself, and of the loss even of this knowledge or certainty of self – the loss of its substance as well as of self; it is the bitter pain which finds expression in the cruel words, 'God is dead'.[2]

The first *real* concept to do justice to the position of man in time and space is neither Being, nor Nothingness, but *Becoming*. This embraces both Being and Nothingness as moments which have been superseded: it is the active effect of the mind, which is aware of the finite nature of its efforts and takes this very seriously; at the same time its energy is constantly being spurred on by the anxiety and pain it experiences at the thought of this finiteness. Man dies, but death brings new life to life; everything man has achieved is swallowed up in nothingness, but it is always being destroyed all over again by means of every new act performed by the consciousness; we lose everything and suffer greatly, but this is the price we must pay if we are to find happiness; we are wrapped up in ourselves, but that is the only way we can force our way through to other people and thus surpass ourselves.

Hegel feels that at this stage all alienation will be eliminated. The consciousness becomes free, it comes to itself. The substance – this is how Hegel puts it – has become subjective. Hegel sets great store by this process of becoming self-conscious; he judges it to be the liberating act *par excellence*. He does not relish the idea of planning some sort of social Utopia: he lived through the collapse of the ideals of the Enlightenment, and that was enough, as far as he was concerned. That is why his philosophy is not in the least concerned with talking his contemporaries into believing exaggerated social claims. In his philosophy all the essential things have already been done. Paradoxically, Hegel became the official Prussian philosopher. His 'God is dead!' is certainly atheistic in so far as it rejects the absolute validity of the Christian faith; but at the same time it corroborates the view that philosophy is essentially a religious attitude: it should be recognized that philosophy has solved the riddle of man and of history. In this, Hegel's 'absolute mind' ousts God from his throne by declaring itself to be a *positive* philosophy. But we do not have to wait long before radical criticism of this view is voiced.

4

Soon after Hegel's death, Ludwig Feuerbach was discerning enough to discover the flaw in his criticism of religion. Hegel's 'absolute mind' is a consciousness which has stepped beyond the limits of its creative radius and has finished up by identifying itself with itself. Now it is confronted with the whole vast emptiness of infinity, as

God was on the seventh day of creation. Feuerbach feels that this is merely a philosophical refinement of theology.

But he, too, does not succeed in avoiding the temptation of religion. Against the idea of the mind, Feuerbach puts forward man as a natural being, a natural creature made of flesh and blood. He rejects Hegel's incorporeal subject as an insubstantial abstraction. The process of overcoming alienation reaches its height in Feuerbach's philosophy in *love*.

The first concrete characteristic which differentiates man from other creatures, the first principle underlying the process of acquiring an individual identity, and the first anthropological relationship, is sex. This is where the terms 'I' and 'you' begin. Feuerbach does not see love as a mere relationship, however, but as a bond: in the first instance the dual 'ego' is a reciprocal thing, an object of passion and longing, an object which we first want to acquire for ourselves, so as to make it into a subject. It is clear that this is possible if every 'ego' relinquishes its subjective identity in favour of every other 'ego', and is prepared for the sake of the other to become its object. But because this giving up of the self is a reciprocal process, each 'ego', by surrendering itself, absorbs the other 'ego' into itself, makes it its property, while it purely and simply gives up its own subjectivity. Thus in the act of love each of the two partners is constantly and increasingly becoming an object and an 'ego', and then being eliminated again; in this way they overcome their remoteness from each other and their unfamiliarity, and penetrate each other. Sexuality is only one fractional part of this infringement of subjectivity; it involves transcending oneself and is at the same time an act of acquisition. This is the basis of morality.

Why then dost thou shrink from naming the nature of God by its true name? Evidently, only because thou hast a general horror of things in their truth and reality; because thou lookest at all things through the deceptive vapours of mysticism.[3]

Feuerbach sees love as the sphere in which a material bond is forged, a *religio* which has been realized, and thus also a genuine religion. When man loves he becomes a God to the other person.

All this means is that in the love relationship, we find our own being in the other person, in the 'you': our anthropological perfection, which we had been unable to attain, embody or 'objectify' up to then. And equally we ourselves become a God for this other person by creating a human being. Physical love results in a man being born.

At this point Feuerbach begins his criticism of religion, which is directed at the Christian version of religion. Religion has shrouded in mysticism something which has its origin and beginning in the physical love relationship. The connection between man and God is exclusively a connection between man and himself, between man and his own essential being; though admittedly this essential being is encountered as another being, a strange being, to whom he awards the highest marks of his species. The religious man is totally unaware that he has projected himself into God. That is precisely the essence of the religious experience: as man is, so is his God. The conclusion is that it is not God who has created man, but man who has created God; on the other hand, of course, it also means that in our eagerness to accept a specific model for God, we also obtain a statement about His creator, man. Theology is always a form of anthropology veiled in mysticism. But – unlike love – religion as taken over by theology is not only a way of couching actual bonds in mystical terms, for it also makes man poorer. For as the God he creates becomes more perfect, so man himself becomes correspondingly less perfect; in making his God very much richer, he makes himself very much poorer. And even more than that: if man objectifies his own being in God by transforming it into a fictitious subject, he himself becomes the object of this subject and hands himself over to it to do as it likes with him. If God is all-powerful, we are powerless.

For Feuerbach, religion involves a degrading alienation. That is why any criticism of 'theologized' religion – which is at bottom also a criticism of all types of idealism – eliminates this alienation and leads man back to himself, to his natural being. The veil of mysticism, alienation, the demand for absolute belief, idealism – all these have been destroyed. We are on the threshold of anthropological materialism.

5

What a long way we are now from the Enlightenment, now that the non-religious consciousness has grasped the fact that anthropology can betray the secret of theology! In its search for that essence with which it could understand mankind fully, it gradually learns that the love-relationship does not lead it into the ideal realm of morality. Yes, it is a realm where lust holds sway; but at the same time 'in this relationship is sensuously revealed, reduced to an observable fact, the extent to which human nature has become nature for man', or – which comes to the same thing – 'how far his *natural* behaviour has become *human*'.[4] The sphere of intimacy which he enters still does not guarantee, in its fervour – which is dependent on chance – that 'the other person, as a person, has become one of his needs' and also he has not as yet furnished any proof in it to show 'to what extent he is in his individual existence at the same time a social being'. When he leaves the gardens of love and returns to the wide world, he observes that neither he nor the other person are abstract beings enthroned in bliss somewhere outside this world, but rather they both stand at the point of intersection of social relationships which make an appeal to their subjectiveness.

These ideas originated with Marx, and he knew that if we clip the wings of religion until it is merely anthropology, we are not taking it back *ad fontes* as much as we should. Man is not merely human *nature*, but also *human* nature, the result of an evolutionary leap forward. So we must expect to find the origins of religious theories in the sort of society where material relations between people have been turned upside down, and this topsy-turvy situation has been codified. In that case, religion represents a general attempt to interpret these relations which have been put under taboo; in view of these relations, religion represents a subjective human need. It is indeed the only sphere in which man can realize himself as a man – even if this realization is purely fictitious – in which he can live out his human existence in the bloodless inadequacy of a dream:

Religious suffering is at the same time an *expression* of real suffering and a *protest* against real suffering. Religion is the sigh of the oppressed creature, the sentiment of a heartless world, and the soul of soulless conditions. It is the *opium* of the people.[5]

Marx's concept of religious suffering originally had nothing in common with the view that religion is primitive and obscure. Admittedly, Marx was aware that there are religious ideas abroad which are both childishly naïve and obscurely fanciful. But he was opposed to the arrogance of the Enlightenment. His idea of religion as opium was the diametrical opposite of the rationalist interpretation. What he means to say is that as long as the material, economic and social relationships which keep men apart persist, the only way the oppressed man can live in such conditions is to create his own realm of relationships which transcend his wretched situation. Religion offers him the means of putting this transcendence into practice for himself: in this way, he begins to put faith and hope in poetic justice; he rises above this satanic world by means of his personal piety, and by leading a life of self-abnegation which is a model of how a man *should* live, an exception from the general rule. But the individual morality which ensues is really a false solution; by behaving as a man in non-human circumstances, he creates the illusion that these circumstances do not come into it at all. What he is really doing is escaping into religion. And without his being able to do anything about it, his escape ranks with other types of escapism, so that the fanatic, the prostitute, the alcoholic are all his illegitimate brothers and sisters.

Marx criticizes any escape which takes the form of a fiction, any opium, not merely the opium of religion. Religion does at any rate have the advantage of being an articulate and institutionalized form of escapism: this means that a critical analysis of religion must form the starting-point of a criticism of this world in general, and of politics. One runs the risk of misunderstanding Marxist atheism entirely, and vulgarizing it, if one picks out no more than the need for a criticism of religion and sets aside all other forms of fictitious escape, simply because they are not specifically religious. If we look at it in this light, modern society is more religious than it owns up to being. Admittedly, its religiosity is often highly primitive. But

Marx was also aware of yet another connection between religion and the factual world: escape represents a negative, passive and passive-making form of criticism of social miseries. That is why it falls down at a certain point: the human values in which the unhappy consciousness takes refuge come across unbearable circumstances. The religious consciousness is provoked into action and begins to protest. This is a protest voiced via the intercession of religion, and it is staged on the level of this intercession. At first, the misery of life on earth appears to the believer to be a distortion of religion. The struggle provoked by this protest appears to him to take the form of a fight for a righteous order in the Biblical sense. But the religious motivation does not alter the fact that, in the last analysis, the material foundations of the force of alienation are affected in this clash, although not as forcefully or as directly as they would be if the conflict were waged by the class which can see what is really happening, because their vision is not shrouded in a religious haze.

Marx therefore differentiates between religion as the expression of suffering and religion as protest against suffering; this is exceedingly important from the point of view of his methodology. It forces us to undertake a concrete analysis of every single religious attitude that has been held throughout history: to adopt a method of differentiation which is the only possible basis for a concrete policy: with whom, against whom, and how? Marx's criticism of religion cannot therefore end up either by having man overruling religion in the realm of acts made by the pure consciousness, for himself alone, nor with his doing this with the help of administrative methods. If 'illusory happiness' is to be eliminated, man must transcend the circumstances which foster such illusions every day. Criticism of religion is therefore 'the embryonic criticism of this vale of tears of which religion is the halo ... Thus the criticism of Heaven is transformed into the criticism of earth, the criticism of religion into the criticism of law, and the criticism of theology into the criticism of politics.' [6] One must simply note that criticism of religion is not an end in itself, as far as Marx is concerned: it is not anti-theistic, not directed against God. Marx believes that the various religions (and he interprets them in concrete terms as the Jewish religion, the Christian religion, etc.) always contain a specific concept of man as a social being. It is up to the critic of religion to unmask this concept, to decode its religious coding, and to lift it clear, so that we can see which are the real human needs and interests that lie hidden behind the ostensible ones. As soon as the champions of the various different religions begin to accept their creeds as stages in the development of the human mind, 'snake skins which have been cast off by history, and man as the snake who clothed himself in them',[7] then the religious differences between them will become less important as the actual differences come to light: they will see that as men they are situated in a specific *political* community. They will not feel that the most important question is how they are going to get rid of religion, but rather how they can realize themselves as men in the concrete framework of economic and political relationships. Marx defines this problem as the conflict between political emancipation and human emancipation, or – more concretely – as the conflict between society made up of citizens and the actual state. As long as this conflict recurs repeatedly – and it will continue to do so as long as the state exists as a special force – the struggle for self-realization within the framework of a political community will also have another side to it in religious and pseudo-religious phenomena. Marx comments – and we can observe this today – that in these circumstances the differences between the various religions will become less important, that Christianity will no longer be a question of Christianity, but of religion in general, the idea of God, whichever religion or ideology it happens to be expressed in. A political society does not get at the heart of the existence of religion just by emancipating itself from its clutches. It does certainly annul the privileges of religion, but by excluding religion as a private realm from the sphere of political distinctions, it ostensibly transforms it into a political matter. So it becomes a universal centre of attraction wherever politics have not yet dug down to the depths of *human* emancipation.

Marx set forth these observations in his essay *On the Jewish Question*. They do not allow the Marxist atheist to break off his critical study of religion at the point where the social relationships which underlie the religious ideas begin to come to light; still less so, if religion becomes in reality a 'non-political' affair within the political structure. The rise or fall of religiosity acts as a sort of barometer by which he can judge the success or failure of his political commitment to the task of emancipating his fellow-men. After all, we don't blame the barometer if it shows bad weather, so there is no reason why the spread of religion should lead us to suppress it by artificial means. We must ask ourselves the following question: which are the places in our practical schemes, where a citizen of our state cannot translate his needs into reality as a man? If we do not ask this question with any idea of creating a Utopia, we will also be aware that the roots of religion do not only lie in the antagonism of economic interests, so that they die away when these interests are eliminated; they also feed on the conflicts between the interests of the citizen and the power of the state. It is virtually certain that we will go on living in social conditions which foster religion for a long time to come.

Man will accept that his own strength is a social strength, and will not be allowed to separate it from himself as an alien *political* strength; *only then* will he be able to engineer his *human* emancipation. The spiritual value of this emancipation lies in the fact that he will be able to see without religion. This means that being a Marxist atheist is not just one other thing that makes the Communist stand out, a sort of extra. Nor is it merely a partial definition, or an ideological standpoint which is quite different from all other standpoints. It is the original dimension of his spiritual equipment. Free of all illusions about his status and resisting them with every step he takes, he has in his mind's eye an image of man as a being who wants to lead his life as a man. He is always asking himself over and over again for an act which will be able to cope with this desire. He is not buoyed up by any celestial hopes, but he experiences all the horror and glory of life, with all its hopes and disappointments. He tries to change the face of history, but he is often unjustly punished by history for his courage, without being certain that there will be any final justice. He senses his wretchedness. But in spite of this he steps forward to fight for a cause which he knows to be imperfect and incapable of ever reaching perfection.

And he never thinks – it never even crosses his mind – that it is in this that his human greatness lies.

6

Up to now no detailed history of atheism has been available to enable us to trace the way the Marxist pattern for atheist consciousness has been put into practice in the labour movement. But we can hardly suppose that this pattern was as far-reaching as Marx wanted it to be on the level of political reflection right from the outset. It is not possible to reflect on the fate of Marxist atheism unless we see it in the context of the concrete historical forms taken by the class war, which the labour movement has been waging since the middle of the nineteenth century. Unless we are the sort of people to whom the sterile purity of an idea means more than practical action which is able to reform life altogether, we will not regret the fact that atheism has not always been up to the standard of Marx. But this practical action always progresses along highly tortuous paths.

At the time of the First International, Marxism was one view among many others within the labour movement; it seems relatively certain that views on atheism different from those held by Marxism were in operation at the time, and indeed had the upper hand. The proletariat was virtually without any rights at all in the bourgeois state, and they felt disinherited and homeless in bourgeois society; this inevitably led, on the one hand, to an elementary plebeian anti-clericalism, and on the other hand to blasphemous forms of atheism, just as in the proletariat concepts of Socialism and Communism were being formed which were not far off being views of an ethical, ethical-cum-religious or heretical-cum-chiliastic nature. And we will certainly have to admit that these views were spiritually closer in spirit to the revolutionary ideas than a petit-bourgeois concept of socialism which is totally utilitarian.

Anti-clerical tendencies within the labour movement obviously increased in the countries where the bourgeoisie was waging a *Kulturkampf* against the Church. This was intended to overthrow the feudal claims of the prelates. In the process, a wave of 'Enlightenment' atheism was washed up from time to time, this time on the part of the ruling bourgeoisie, but more in the form of political demagogism. Yet in so doing it also compelled leading Catholic circles to start thinking on political lines; and on the other hand, this type of atheism was obviously not without influence on the proletariat, where the legacy of the Enlightenment philosophers was for ever strengthening resistance to the chains of clerical dogmatism. In this, anti-clericalism fairly often joined forces with nationalism and chauvinism. In the last twenty-five or so years of the nineteenth century, bourgeois anti-clericalism in Germany threw all its weight into fighting against the Catholic Church in the name of German national Protestantism; and it developed into part of an attack on the 'three internationals', the red, the black and the yellow. In Austria-Hungary anti-Catholic atheists allied themselves with national attempts at achieving independence. In traditionally Catholic Italy, the anti-ecclesiastical resistance which had once accompanied the revolutionary romanticism of the *Carabinieri* and Garibaldi's 'Redshirts' gradually died out. It is difficult to see how the experiences undergone by civic society could have failed to influence the labour movement and its atheistic way of thinking.

In the countries which did not manage to get their civil revolution over and done with in time, which staged it in a tentative, cowardly, inconsistent and patchy manner coloured by their fear of the proletariat, the compromise in the relationship between the bourgeoisie and feudalism was always masked by the fact that they flaunted a limited form of anti-clericalism and revived the Enlightenment, even though it was already veering in the direction of decadent irrationality.

However we judge the preponderance of plebeian anti-clericalism in the labour movement today, it was an elevated sentiment even in this form, and was produced by ideas and practical currents quite different from those which motivated the anti-clericalism of the bourgeoisie and the petty bourgeoisie. From time to time, it is true, it gave way to the other type of anti-clericalism, but it was always one step ahead; at least this was true as long as it did not relinquish the idea of changing conditions within the bourgeoisie.

Engels, in particular, did a good deal to foster this spiritual attitude. At any rate, the bourgeois/aristocratic atheism embodied by men such as Friedrich Nietzsche remained entirely foreign to the labour movement. It would be difficult to find a more venomous attitude against Christianity anywhere in literature. And yet this resolutely anti-Christian attitude is unacceptable. It reflects, unintentionally, the mood of self-reproach which beset the enlightened rationalists when they admitted how disappointed they were at the début reason had made in history, and sought a scapegoat on to which they could transfer their own guilt. Their hatred was directed first and foremost against Christianity; they saw it as a sort of pestilence which had contaminated everything with which it came into contact, removing any value it might have: it had debased the clear virile spirit of antiquity, which had been guided by fine instincts; it had infected the Renaissance and from the outset had wormed its way into it like a germ, causing it to decay progressively. Nietzsche saw its attempt to transform man the predator into a tame and slave-like domestic animal as an indication of its pernicious influence. Today – he proclaims – we may no longer conceal the truth, as the philistines do, but must voice it publicly – the future belongs to the strong, the predator, the superman. God is long since dead. It is now time that he was publicly buried.

Just as de Sade once exposed the seamy side of the ideals of 'sound' common sense, so Nietzsche ripped off the chaste robes of unhealthy reason and promoted the pathology of reason to a basic principle of life and society. Popular anti-clericalism could find a whole lot of arguments against Christianity in Nietzsche; but the spirit and general outlook of his work is alien to genuine atheism as embodied in Marxism. They have never found an echo in the labour movement instigated by Marxism.

The revolutionary circumstances in Russia did a good deal to intensify anti-clerical tendencies within the labour movement and Marxist atheism. The outlook of the Russian Orthodox Church had all along differed from the outlook of the Christian Churches in Europe. At the beginning of the twentieth century, Tsarist Russia was the most reactionary empire in Europe, and the Orthodox Church was the most reactionary of the Christian Churches. The power of the state and the power of the Church belonged together as if they were the right and left hands of the same body. Since Tsarist Russia deliberately kept the populace illiterate, the Orthodox Church was well below the cultural level of the other Christian Churches. This meant that the struggle of the Russian revolutionaries to overthrow tsardom inevitably ended, whether they wanted it to or not, in violent anti-clericalism, although they could not get round the fact that the Orthodox Church had a widespread influence on the masses. Similarly, the Narodniki Movement embraced radicalism and anti-clericalism and also contained elements of the Enlightenment. Our knowledge of history tells us how this movement ended. The Marxist Party founded by Lenin knew that the road to emancipation did not lead in that direction. Their main preoccupation lay elsewhere. But as things are, it is highly likely that they too will not be able to escape altogether the stamp of a superficial anti-clericalism and a far too harsh rationalism; this is all the more likely because, even among the ranks of the avantgarde of the revolutionary movement, a mood of disloyalty and scepticism began to creep in after the defeat of the first Russian Revolution, and men began to search for God. Lenin's guiding rules concerning the relationship between socialism and religion amount to a demand for Church and state to sever all connections; he differentiates between religion as a private affair, and the connection between religion and the socialist state, but he does not think of it as something which is of no consequence whatsoever inside the Marxist Party; in the specific circumstances prevailing in Russia, these rules have the same outstanding political importance as his conception of militant atheism, which is based on the findings and views of scientists.

We really cannot shut our eyes to the fact that Lenin starts from a very concrete consideration of the situation: given the circumstances in Russia, the separation of Church and state meant that the Orthodox Church as a component part of the political power of the tsardom was to be wiped out. But to eliminate the Church from political life automatically meant – again, given the situation in Russia – ousting it from the life of the ordinary citizen: Russia was so fantastically backward compared with the development of capitalism in the rest of Europe that there was absolutely no question of a civic society in the Marxist sense emerging (i.e. a system of bourgeois-democratic institutions to counterbalance the bourgeois state). There was nothing else but for religion to become a totally private matter in its relationship to the socialist state, since the first duty of the state was to develop democratic institutions for a *socialist* society made up of citizens. This type of attitude was produced by a profound respect for the historical framework within which the Russian people had been living for centuries. Lenin was aware that religious consciousness belongs to the sphere of one's outlook on life, and therefore also to the sphere of highly personal decisions about one's life, the motivation of which is guided by traditions, cultural and psychological factors, and one's level of education. That is precisely why he demanded categorically that the avant-garde worker should adopt a deliberate and militant materialism, a pronounced and clear attitude to religion, and create the extremely necessary propaganda for scientific knowledge.

While the working classes were waging their long battle, civic institutions were set up in the countries of Western Europe; and nowhere else had there been such an absolute identification of the Church with the power of the bourgeoisie as in Tsarist Russia. One result of this was that Christianity, too, was more discriminating politically and spiritually; this meant that in Russia rather different prerequisites began to be evolved for the political attitude of the Communist Parties to the Churches, and for the development of Marxist atheism. These began to make themselves felt in the practical political policies of the different parties, both at the time of the popular front, and also after the Second World War, in the early years of the development of popular democracy in those countries where the working class had seized power. So revolutionary Russia had to go through its own 'French Revolution' in its relationship to the Church. Lenin's policies were admittedly distorted for many years, and this probably caused the Russians to prolong this phase far longer than they should have.

It can hardly be doubted that this, too, had an influence on the special brand of anti-clericalism which made itself felt in the Communist movement in Western Europe in the post-war years.

The chief blame for this must rest with the militant anti-Communist and anti-Soviet attitude adopted by the Christian Churches of Western Europe for almost half a century. Various motives combined to produce this attitude; one of these was the fact that some of Marx's writings – works which were essential to his view of atheism – were not published until many decades after his death. This delay complicated the development of Marxist atheism.

In all this we can see the 'pure ideas' being debased; and on behalf of these ideas we can ridicule or blame the anti-clerical attitude. We will come across both these factors in the two opposing ideological camps; but they merely represent an attempt which should not be taken seriously – in fact it is essentially a non-political attempt – to find some way of approaching the historical ambiguity of Marxist atheism. But this is not the way: what one needs to do is to respect the efforts of the revolutionary labour movement to attain emancipation. In so doing, one creates a climate of understanding for the obstacles which have checked their progress, and a feeling of admiration for the doggedness with which the atheist movement has managed to surmount these obstacles. And even those attempts which went totally astray will no longer seem ridiculous or futile.

That is the right way of taking a close look at ourselves and at our history.

Marxist atheism will be the richer for it: its adherents know now that it is more than mere anti-clericalism, more even than the sophistry of the Enlightenment. They know that however much they strain their vocal chords they will never manage to overthrow the Churches; and even the combined forces of reason will never manage to overthrow belief. They discover that their atheism is the spiritual basis of this movement which has grasped fully and completely that man is totally on his own on the earth with no one to protect him; at the same time there are many possibilities open to him. They know that we are nothing, but that we want to be everything: not in the divine sense, but in the totally human sense.

Footnotes

1) Kosík: *Die Dialektik des Konkreten*, 1967.

2) G. W. F. Hegel: *The Phenomenology of Mind*, translated by J. B. Baillie, Sonnenschein, 1910, Vol. II, Section VII, part C. 'Revealed Religion', p. 762.

3) Ludwig Feuerbach: *The Essence of Christianity*, translated from second German edition by Marian Evans, Trübner & Co., n.d.

4) This sentence and the following sentences are an almost word-by-word paraphrase of Marx's *Economic and Philosophical Manuscripts* (*Nazionalökonomie und Philosophie*), Third Manuscript, in *Early Writings*, translated by T. B. Bottomore, Watts, 1963, p. 154.

5) Karl Marx: *Contribution to the Critique of Hegel's Philosophy of Right: Introduction* in *Early Writings*, pp. 43 f.

6) Karl Marx: ibid., p. 44.

7) Karl Marx: *On the Jewish Question*, loc. cit., p. 5.

3

ATHEIST PROFILES

... The comrade has a positive relationship to the institutions of the people's democracy. His sincerity, gaiety and sociability make him popular in his collective unit. He is married, with two children, and leads an orderly family life. He has duly come to terms with the religious question. We therefore recommend that he should be appointed to the post you have in mind for him.

Many of us remember very clearly this stereotyped formula, which was used for all executive posts during a certain period. To be religious was thought at that time to be a sort of character defect, and it was certainly thought of as an incriminating characteristic from the political point of view. This phrase, which smoothed things out so neatly, stated the end-result with much satisfaction, but no one was interested in knowing what had happened before. That was why the idea could arise and become firmly entrenched that in our countries atheism was spreading as a socially significant factor, which was in the process of maturing and standardizing our outlook on life.

This view is basically correct. It was endorsed by a recent sociological investigation into the state of religiosity today; though at the same time this did also ruthlessly refute the self-satisfaction of those who held it. It did away with the idea that the atheists form a single, uniform, spiritually and intellectually compact group of all those people who do not believe in God. And as a result, this investigation did not even set itself the task of testing how deep their atheistic conviction went.

The comrade has duly come to terms with the religious question. So, he is an atheist.

Is he an atheist? What exactly does being an atheist mean anyway? How did each of us who think of ourselves as such come to be atheists? What criterion should we use? and what is the atheist like?

Now this is a highly personal matter. There are millions of different answers to it in our country. Each of these is unique, irreproducible, and highly intimate; incidents which can be told in the form of a biography, as personal confessions, as a novel.

Until recently the sole criterion for distinguishing theists from atheists was to be found in statistics provided by the religious evidence: i.e. whether the person in question attended divine service regularly; whether he participated in the main Church ceremonies (baptisms, confirmations, weddings and burials); the percentage of children who were enrolled by their parents for religious instruction. Over and above anything the registry offices and other official civic documents could provide in the way of data concerning people's membership of any one Church, the only way of determining what sort of attitude a citizen held was to ask him for a personal statement. It was tacitly taken for granted that all those citizens who did not appear in such statistics were atheists.

Sociological investigations at home and abroad have demolished superficial and inaccurate theories of this kind. More precise yardsticks were used, the quality of the religious or atheistic conviction was considered, and in this way it became necessary to introduce a large group of 'don't knows' in between the atheists and the believers. And even if the sole aim of our investigation was to establish the standard and growth-rate of religiosity, and was not concerned at all with the standard of atheistic conviction, it did nevertheless bring to light some views which make some sort of distinctions necessary within the atheist group as well.

Other investigations, once again both abroad and at home, take this discrimination even further. They show, for instance, that a theistic or atheistic conviction can extend to people holding differing social or political attitudes: that they have a conflicting effect on value-judgements; that the social behaviour of theists and atheists is different. It was discovered that there was a correlation between performance of religious duties and attitude to money; it was recognized that a fall-off in religious faith is coupled in a certain social milieu with an increase in the number of people who believe in the future of Communism; but it is also coupled with a fall-off in prudishness and more liberal views on sexual intercourse. It is recognized that an increase in religious conviction also strengthens specific attitudes to ethical values; but it also increases the tendency to conservatism in social and political matters.

But even these criteria, although far-reaching and more accurate, still cannot go further than a certain point. They will be able to establish how the atheist differs from the theist, and provide a reliable description of any such differences. But they cannot tell us why they differ. At best, they can help us to obtain an insight into the historical development of atheistic conviction.

The only way to produce an analysis of the atheistic consciousness is to undertake a whole series of special sociological investigations conducted according to an overall philosophical plan.

The phenomenon of the atheistic consciousness has not so far been examined in the whole complexity of its existence, its emergence and the various transformations it has undergone (investigations into forms of belief do exist, but none has ever been made into atheism), nor are there any statements available about the internalization of the values held by the atheistic consciousness. We do not know whether people become atheists today primarily under the influence of exogenous or endogenous factors, whether they become atheists by working on themselves or on other people, whether the atheist arrives at his own definition, primarily by adapting himself, by conforming, or by undertaking an authentic critical and ideological re-moulding of his whole outlook.[1]

What is needed is a study of the connection between a change in the economic and social structure and the formation of various different types of atheism; what is needed is a discriminating idea of how the most varied ethical, axiological and philosophical systems or attitudes are integrated into the over-all atheistic conviction, and what sort of spiritual differences this causes; what is also needed is some graphic information about the inner life of an atheist; what is needed is . . .

The comrade has duly come to terms with the religious question.

In spite of all these things which are still needed, we want to try to rough out a hypothetical sketch of what this type of statement can mean.

2

An atheistic conviction is the product of reasoning alone, even if it is a form of consciousness, and indeed, in the best cases, of self-consciousness. One is not an atheist or a theist by birth. One becomes one or the other by virtue of the circumstances into which one is born and which one has undertaken or taken upon oneself; and this depends on the way in which one has consciously made them one's own, has 'internalized' them.

When religiously-minded sociologists or non-religiously-minded ones are unanimous in stating that there is what amounts to a 'religious crisis', a long-term historical process in the course of which society has been turning away from religion, a process accelerating all the time, there is no question at first of whether they judge this process to be positive, and see it as a step forward, or negative, and a tragedy. All they can do is help us to look into the objective causes underlying this acceleration.

The spread of atheism goes back to the process of industrialization, irrespective of whether this happened under capitalism or under socialism. Industrialization loosened the original organic ties, the threads of a life which was deeply rooted in the earth, in a single natural milieu to which the agricultural worker was totally committed. A regular rhythm of life, which was not subject to any dynamic forces and revolved in the same natural cycles, which determined the regularly recurring cycles of procreation and divided life into day and night: all this was first of all turned upside down by the new industrialization, and then eventually destroyed altogether. The Christian faith was still – as it had been since the darkest days of medieval feudalism – a spiritual reflection of this cyclical pattern of life, and also provided its cultural structure. The ecclesiastical year – the regular recurrence of the advent ceremonies, the festival of Christ's birth, his presentation in the Temple, his secret and resigned preparation in the wilderness, his public activity, his persecution and crucifixion, his death, his ascension into Heaven, and the descent of the Holy Ghost – formed a second layer of consciousness which gave a point to the cycle of work and the cycle of nature. The cycle of individual life, from birth to death, was played out within this over-all pattern of recurrence, and was clearly circumscribed by the wider concentric circles.

All this was pushed into the background of social occurrences by the process of industrialization. The Church cycle did remain relatively stable in rural areas. Practical politics confirmed in the most diverse ways that the most progressive parties, which embraced anti-clericalism far too fervently, got into difficulties when they tried to set their agricultural policy in motion, and vice versa. Industrialization not only effected far-reaching changes in the social structure and altered the relative positions of the social classes and strata, but also replaced the static, cyclic rhythm of life with a dynamic, forward-looking, rhythm, spiralling upwards and growing faster and faster all the time. But over and above this it also organized life completely differently, according to a series of basic principles, none of which could be taken as definitive. These changes resulted in completely different relationships to one's homeland, to one's birthplace, to the earth and the soil, to nature, to travelling, to the family, to one's wife, to one's children, to one's neighbours ... They put a different value on youth, adulthood and old age, on money and property; they created new longings, new desires, new motivations, different behaviour. People now are slotted into the world in a totally different way; they are compelled to live differently and to die differently.

A God conceived as a static being, static dogmas, a static ecclesiastical year – *agrarian religion* loses its potential for influencing people as industrialization advances. In the towns, particularly in the big cities, where the social and cultural structure is after all quite different, this type of religion seems completely foreign and is met with apathy. This does not mean that in certain circumstances it lost all its appeal: it can often still be found in a *cache* of romantic memories of the beautiful stability of organic cycles; these come to the surface now and then, when people have become harassed and exhausted, in the form of a yearning for a return to the days of long ago. Another factor is that the Churches are making an effort to adapt themselves to the rhythm of modern life, even though this attempt is nowhere near forceful enough to overcome the consequences of industrialization.

Factory, company, business, office, cinema, sports stadium, Church; streets, traffic, taxis, trams, telephones, radio, television, rapid channels of communication; couplings and feedback; democracy, protests, meeting in public and intimate *tête-à-têtes*, goings-on behind the scenes, strikes, religious gatherings; educational questions, career, business trips, aeroplane, Egypt, New Zealand; war, space-flights, manoeuvres, the U.N., high-level politics, low-level politics, rockets, atom bombs, jazz, revues, pin-ups, alcohol; work, drudgery, day, which turns into night, night, which turns into day, money, rising prices, the standard of living; crimes, murders, catastrophes, damage at sea; longing to escape, attempts to escape; longing for quiet, longing for noise. Another laugh, another cry.

There is no room among all this for a static religion; or only right on the periphery. But this means also that the process of industrialization, the far-reaching change in the structure and rhythm of social life and the life of the individual, creates atheism of itself, along with many other after-effects, as a state of religious apathy and unthinking human consciousness; it creates conditions in which man is already godless the moment he first sees the light of day. If we are right to be convinced that the scientific and technological revolution accelerates this process, then we cannot doubt that a static religion no longer has the slightest chance of survival, and religious apathy will increase at the same rapid pace.

But only a very naïve atheist will see in this a cause for rejoicing. We must in fact ask ourselves to what extent this type of atheism and godlessness is really an asset; or whether it doesn't rather – this may seem paradoxical – signify the loss of all those cultural values which are part of Christianity. We must also ask ourselves to what extent atheism in our country is the product of *our* ideal influence, of *our* ideological effect, i.e. a product of the appeal of Marxist atheism; or whether it should not in fact be classified as a concomitant symptom of a higher level of civilization and industrialization. Thirdly, we must ask ourselves what will take the place, in a world without God, of the role which was formerly performed by static Christianity, and whether Christianity cannot exist any other way than in this static conception; whether it could not perhaps find other models which would correspond far better to the dynamism and needs of our modern way of life.

It would at any rate be very one-sided if we were to seek the reasons for the increase of godlessness – or, to use a common term, the secularization of public and private life – solely in the process of industrialization. The socio-economic situation in any given country also has an unquestionable influence on the spread of atheism, or, to put it the other way, on the growth or decline of religious belief. On the one hand we should recognize in this a long-term trend transforming religious values into non-religious ones: in this respect, capitalism helps to uphold the religious consciousness, whereas the socialist system of society helps to bring about its decline. Sufficiently striking evidence of this can be seen in the difference between two traditionally Catholic countries such as Austria and Poland. But the subjective activity of the ruling political forces and groups has an even stronger influence. It would be utterly wrong to disregard the effect of the Christian-Democratic governments and parties in a number of countries in Western Europe on the stability of the prestige of the various denominations, just as it would also be wrong not to take into account such factors as the influence of the Communist Party, as a leading political force in our country, on the spread and development throughout public life of a campaign for educating people which is governed by atheist theories.

Running parallel to this, there is a whole series of other factors making themselves felt to a greater or lesser degree: the level of education, tradition, the strength of intimate relationships, emotional ties, customs, conventions, psychological references ...

Primitive godlessness, like carefully-thought-out atheism, always embraces several different strata, and in these there is a whole series of focal points and lines of communication; some of these have already been fixed, but others have not yet been defined. But the accumulation of all these factors always leads in the individual to a specific variant on an existing type of atheist conviction.

For the time being a scientific analysis of these different types is not available. We could also do with a sociological explanation which would be able to teach us what proportion of our citizens adheres to each of these types, and tell us about the different variants on the basic types which are represented in our society. And yet a knowledge of these factors is essential if there is to be any point in our efforts to create a spiritual orientation for socialist man, and a spiritual basis for socialism. The next section consists of an attempt to classify the different types of atheism, though this is of a totally hypothetical nature.

3

The practical atheist: a godless man devoid of ideas; a man created by the process of civilization, by the all-pervading secularization of life. Only the trivial elements of concrete events and of history find any echo in him, only those things which are always rapidly changing, like foam on the surface of the sea. World events and politics appear to him as no more than dry facts, as externals, multifarious, contradictory and involved; as far as he is concerned, they are remote, difficult to understand, menacing. He does have a vague idea of whether the general situation is threatening or peaceful or whether the mood is generally placatory. In the whirl of events which follow each other in rapid succession, he loses all sense of the over-all pattern, all feeling for meaning and significance. He either feels ill at ease, or else is apathetic to the whole business. Everything seems so far away and so alien.

The only things which seem to him to be alive and full of importance are his immediate worries. But he cannot work out where 'high-level' politics and history influence and encroach on this personal sphere. He experiences the trivial, stereotyped course of events, which is repeated virtually wholesale, down to the tiniest detail, as a sort of background – generally speaking a thoroughly tedious one – to his search for a mode of existence which fits in with his ambition to be happy.

His attitude to supra-individual values is unthinking, or only vaguely thought out. He accepts socialism without question as an empirical fact of life. He weighs up political changes purely on utilitarian grounds. He does not set much store by ideas.

He is completely apathetic towards religion. He has no conception of God. But he is equally apathetic towards ideological atheism and towards any more demanding form of ideal motivation. He thinks of religion as utter nonsense. He does not think of socialism as utter nonsense, but this is only because it never occurs to him to do so, since he lives under it.

His outlook on life has not been rounded off into a coherent whole. It is pieced together from a variety of vulgar-cum-materialistic views and idealistic attitudes which he has adopted for the sake of convention. He is not at all willing to expose his views, and doesn't like taking any form of risk. He fears the unknown consequences which might ensue. He is egocentric – a mixture of caution and aggressiveness. He weighs up objects, relationships and events from the point of view of their usefulness. What he is in fact is 'practical'.

Admittedly, this sketch must inevitably be abstract. In real life we come across a vast range of variants: they vary according to age, profession, sex, standard of education. They can look very different, ranging from the honestly industrious and sedately snobbish to the crude, uncouth, and socially uprooted.

But whatever the relationship may be between the individual psycho-social traits, the dominant factor is always a utilitarian, pragmatic attitude to life, a deeply ingrained apathy about religious questions, an underdeveloped understanding of the supra-individual motivation underlying one's own actions, a limited capacity for objective reflection and for looking closely at oneself, and a more or less elementary way of reacting to those facts which transcend man and to which he is subject. Interspersed among each of these traits there can of course be various modes of expression which appear to be at variance with the basic melody.

In a modern socialist society which has reached an advanced stage of individual development, the sort of atheism which is devoid of ideas and is purely practical is a negative quantity. We plunge here into a vacuum where there is no God, but no mind either: into a mindlessness which might also be defined as an irrational vacuum which cannot be measured and is not under control. It abhors itself in an elementary way, and is always looking for ways of escaping from itself.

Since this type of atheist is quite incapable of distinguishing between values, since he has never known religion, which has thoroughly pronounced views on such matters, and since he does not recognize any other scale of values, he takes refuge in pseudo-values: i.e. he exchanges real life for play-acting. He acts his way through life, through his quarrels, his loves and his hatreds, and thus transforms reality into a myth.

I know that I am exposing myself to highly emotional criticism if I put forward the view that one such pseudo-religious drug is sports mania. In saying this, what I have in mind is not the perfectly natural interest which can be roused by the dramatic climaxes in sport, nor the excitement, nor the mental relaxation and compensation for the seriousness of life, where the rules are not all laid down in advance and where those who have fallen may well be left lying on the field when the contest is over. I see this mania rather as a sociological phenomenon; I also realize that somewhere in the background there are men who are hard-headed and calculating technicians in their own field. What interests me is the false enthusiasm of the fans, which acts as a drug. They construct a world in which people escape from reality, but then recreate the deplorable aspects of reality by attributing them to a specific group of people – the enemy club, while attributing the desirable ideal aspects of reality to their own club – 'our' club. Thus both aspects are personified. 'Our' club is naturally good, the other club is naturally bad. This means that the individual men who make up the team in concrete terms are not of primary importance; all that really matters is the name of the club, its colours, its flag, its emblems, its symbols. The team is idolized, and implored, and the members joyfully give it both material and moral support. This means that their fanatical admirers see the struggle between the two teams merely as a symbol for *their own* unfought battles, a projection of *their own* non-existent brave deeds, an idealization of *their own* fear of taking real risks. The more cowardly they are when it comes to real fighting, the more aggressive they are behind the barrier. The adversary of their sports club is the fictitious embodiment of their own enemies, and here the fan can shout out loud that the enemies must be slaughtered. The men who play for his own club, toiling on the grass or on the ice, producing record performances, and displaying stupendous body control and exemplary self-discipline, are a manifestation to the enraptured fan in the stands of his own ideal performances, which unfortunately can never be achieved. He is quite prepared to reconcile himself to his own inadequacies; but if the man rushing around on the sports ground, who is supposed to be incorporating 'his qualities' – the virtues which the spectator would love to possess himself – falters, then the spectator is all the more implacable; for it is really himself he is cheering on, himself he is criticizing – but all this is purely fictitious, playful, nebulous, total self-alienation.

In this way the clubs are transformed into crypto-religious *sects*, whose drug is hatred and aggression. The two extremes of sectarianism in the life of the club – enthusiasm and brutality – give away the secret of what this feeble and cowardly subject would do if it came to power. The dangerous rise in the sectarian life of sport, the increase in fan-mania as a fictitious escape from reality and as a drug, can be seen as a symptom of the fact that in the midst of social reality the relationships in which man can really be himself are destroyed. This is in fact the moment to comment that the fanaticism of the sports clubs is merely deputizing for a growing number of crypto-religious sects in our totally irreligious, totally atheistic world.

The non-ideological form of atheism suffers from this instability because it is helpless. It is a prey to the most obscure kinds of superstition, the most illusory passions, the most primitive urges. It is the raw material for every kind of political reaction. It is miles away from cultured religiosity or even from reflective atheism.

On the other hand, this type of atheist surprises us by the greedy way he snaps up anything offered to him, because he is such a total blank. This means that he is constantly waiting for something or someone to come and speak to him as a man. He only *appears* to have a surfeit of pleasures. He is really permanently hungry.

In societies which have reached an advanced stage of industrialization, which have a very high consumption-level, this hunger, although hidden, is always present. Provided that it can be superficially appeased by the acquisition of objects, its true nature does not always come to light: i.e. the practical atheist's longing for something which would enable him to transcend himself, to realize himself more fully, more perfectly. He feels that material possessions supply him with the value which he does not himself possess. A god-fearing man ascribes a supernatural power and perfection to God; the pseudo-religious man who gave up believing in God long ago, or never believed in him at all, does the same with objects, and expects them to help him in his struggle to acquire social prestige. He transforms them into fetishes. He thinks that *having* more means *being* more.

Yet as soon as his hunger has been appeased to such an extent that his standing is above the social average, or as soon as he begins to realize that he is on quite the wrong track, this hunger suddenly emerges in its true colours.

That is the moment when men begin to long anxiously for a human word, for possibilities of expression by means of which the subject can create its own values.

It is there that the cultured forms of religion get their chance. But it also represents a chance for Marxism and Marxist atheism to step in. In a socialist society one should not let this opportunity go by unused. It is essential that this should be realized and the void filled up, if we are to prove that socialism is superior to capitalism.

4

The conformist atheist: he has grasped that atheism is one of the political demands which are made of a known socialist or Communist. He knows, in a rather vague and abstract way, that Marxism also means atheism. Thanks to the general education he has received, he remembers that religion contradicts the views held by scientists. His own experience and his experience in a socialist community has taught him that Churches and religious associations have taken a stand against socialism; he knows from what he sees happening all round him that religion has obstructed the passive adoption of socialism, and even more the active adoption of it. In so far as he is a party member, he knows that his membership is incompatible with his belonging to any Church or with his believing in God. But anyway, for a wide variety of reasons, religion has never been one of the basic values of his life. In so far as he grew up in a family which belonged to one or other of the Christian denominations, he has always experienced religion as something connected with childhood. When he grew up he began to think of religion as no more than an outward convention, a formal structure which contained nothing that was likely to be of any use to him in his own life, nor anything that would be able to make it all that much more complicated. He remains a member of this or that Church through laziness and is entered in the registers as such. Now and then he might even carry on going to Church, but without ever properly grasping what was really going on during divine service. He had a rather vague conception of the fact that Christianity preaches moral principles which are designed to serve the general good and should be taught to children from an early age. That is why he thought in his own mind that it might possibly be a good thing if his children were to attend religious instruction classes. As a rule he had them christened and confirmed, but would attend divine service only very occasionally himself, after he had reached adulthood. He would consult his priest at the other exceptional events in his life, such as a wedding or a funeral, but he did not set much store by this consultation.

It was not until he began to participate actively in political life that he was compelled to make up his mind about his former conventional and formal attitudes and opinions, including the religious question, and this became absolutely necessary when he joined the Communist Party. He had no difficulty in taking his leave of religion. He saw this as a political requirement, but at the same time it did add to his self-respect.

Admittedly there were also some conformist considerations at work, sometimes even fairly strong ones. The new party member realized that it would not be the done thing for him to remain within the community of the Church now that he was a Communist, or to go to church, or to send his children to scripture lessons. There were certainly also some cases where a public break with the Church was purely a question of opportunism.

Conformist atheism is apathetic towards religion. But it is equally apathetic to atheism when it is put forward as an attitude *which is of great significance to society*. The conformist atheist's break with religion in an utterly concrete historical situation is either a personal duty or a demand that has been made of him. As soon as he has met this demand, he considers that the whole matter is over and done with.

His mind is interested in the *practical* questions involved in establishing socialism. As far as he is concerned, atheism is a peripheral matter. So he has no further thoughts about all the urgent things that he must do *now* as an atheist. He does not see atheism as a genuine dimension of the consciousness; he does not think in the long term.

That is why he does not see socialism and Communism as *being* a historical problem, but rather thinks of them as *having* greater or lesser empirical problems.

Conformist atheism is still not sufficiently thought out among socialists and Communists. It is a form of atheism which does not look beyond itself, and has no precise knowledge either of itself or of its potential.

5

Anti-clericalism and anti-theism, unlike conformist atheism, are opposed to religion – i.e. to the Christian Churches – on principle. A specific ideological and highly emotional motivation underlies their attitude.

The anti-clericalists see the Churches and their representatives as highly dangerous enemies of the human race in general and socialism in particular. They can draw on extensive historical material in which the Churches are represented as the forces of darkness, of the worst type of reaction, as obstacles in the path of any form of progress, skilfully marking time and constantly adapting themselves, so as to ensure that their immense wealth and their positions of power remain untouched. They have at their finger-tips a wide range of historical evidence which gives them the right to this opinion, starting from the horrors of the medieval Inquisition, via the subtle and destructive demagogy addressed to the working class, right down to the point where the Fascists had their weapons blessed, crimes against humanity were passed over in silence, and a venomous anti-Soviet and anti-Communist attitude made itself widely felt in the Churches.

They are ready at every opportunity to make disclosures concerning the political activities of the clergy, and go to tremendous lengths to collect documents which demonstrate their activity against the progressive forces at work in the world; they have a detailed knowledge of the economic and political ties which bind the clericalists to the imperialist powers, and carefully record every case of hostility on the part of the Church dignitaries, so as to make good use of it in their indictment.

And yet this is still not Marxist atheism. Not because their revelations are wide of the mark, nor because their deliberate intention is to twist or distort the facts. Even if anti-clericalism remains strictly objective, even if its catalogue of the execrable deeds performed by the Church is absolutely accurate, and the revelations it makes can pass muster by any kind of scientific criteria, even then it is still inadequate as far as the Marxist is concerned, and on several counts.

The fundamental flaw in anti-clericalism concerns its methods: it proceeds *a priori* from the assumption that Christianity was always anti-progressive, still is and therefore always will be. But they never really ask themselves why this should be. Since they do not examine their basic thesis sufficiently critically, they think that every action performed by the Christian religion and its Churches is, without exception, reactionary – but by treating all the Churches' actions indiscriminately, they are also being unhistorical. They are not capable of making any concrete historical differentiation between the various actions; and the reprehensible deeds performed by the Church and its retrogressive policies strengthen them in their opinion. But anything which does not fit in with this judgement is dismissed as mere tactics, as a highly subtle and cunning form of demagogy, and they are incapable of analysing whether their accusations are pertinent or whether they are untenable. The statements they make about Christianity are steeped in ideology, which makes it impossible for them to treat it without prejudice.

One concomitant phenomenon of anti-clericalism – or perhaps it is merely a variant on it – is *anti-theism*. Just as the anti-clerically-minded are haunted by the activities of the Churches, so the anti-theist rises at the idea of a God who exists outside himself in the ideal world of the believer. He sees this concept as a mere phantom produced by the priests, but he also thinks of it as such an utterly ludicrous idea that its champions cannot be classified as anything but a special type of intellectual primitives.

Yet anti-theism is also unacceptable to the Marxist. The anti-theist's thinking is in line with the rationalism of the Enlightenment and the inadequate philosophical reasoning on which this type of rationalism is based. Since he will accept nothing as real unless it is rational, all the illusions produced by 'sound common sense' become reality. As far as he is concerned, reality is reflected in the concepts adopted by mechanistic materialism or naturalism. But this results in his worshipping things which are purely of this world: matter, nature, reason, or a specific social situation are seen as counter-balancing and contrasting with the God professed by the various religions.

The anti-clericalist and the anti-theist are quite unaware that in so doing they are unintentionally allying themselves with their opponents, the real clergy, who naturally take full advantage of this: they make things far too easy for them. With all their revelations they help them to decide before it is too late what must be changed and what had better be covered up and kept dark.

6

The abstract humanist atheist: his atheism generally results from his having found a way out of a personal religious crisis which had affected his whole existence. His belief in God, in whom he had up to now found the redeeming values of mankind, has now been shattered. There may be several reasons for this: it may be that he treated his belief mechanically and it did not hold its own against the various conflicting opinions he came across in life; he may have undergone such terrible personal or supra-personal tragedies that he could no longer reconcile this with believing in God; this type of person may have also worked his way through to a different philosophical concept of life, in which there was no room for God. In each of these cases, the religious values of his inner life cannot be disposed of with a mere wave of the hand or simply left out of account altogether. They must be overcome in a violent struggle in which all the pros and cons must be weighed against each other all over again, in an inner conflict the upshot of which is that he completely reconstructs his spiritual structure; in deliberately choosing this course of action, he is aware of what the consequences will be, at least those which affect his own existence.

An act of choice of this kind often takes place against a background of violent conflicts in the family and with his friends, and is accompanied by decisions which often have long-term or even permanent consequences, both spiritual and practical.

This type of atheistic conviction is never indifferent to religion. But it does not give in to its suggestions. It is imbued inwardly with the knowledge that a religious conviction contains values which can give strength and consolation to the believer, and that it possesses a whole series of moral and universally human advantages which distinguish the true Christian from the vulgar atheist. But he is also familiar with the inner mechanism of religious emotions, and is capable of observing them without prejudice: the psychology of faith has no secrets from the humanistic atheist.

Unlike the anti-theist, infantile types of religious conviction do not rattle him, because he knows that Christianity is capable of offering solace which puts new heart into people in a wide range of eventualities, beginning with the simplest type – which appeals to the emotions by means of images – down to solace on a very high intellectual level. He is at any rate aware that such consolation, although certainly highly effective, is unfortunately a mere illusion. The only thing which really sickens him is spiritual emptiness, whether it is religious or irreligious.

If we look at it from the positive angle, his atheism is based on one of the philosophies derived from Socrates, or on an eclectic mixture of such philosophies which corresponds to his inner needs, and to his views on what man should really be like and what sort of values he should believe in.

He builds up his *Weltanschauung*, drawing on his own experiences and his reading, as an utterly personal practical philosophy. It contains elements of both Stoicism and Epicureanism, a dash of modern scepticism and a few materialistic ideas, a reflection of those states and feelings which are now over and done with in his life, a frank appreciation of aesthetic pleasures, a marked awareness of his own personality, compassion for others, or alternatively the opposite conviction – i.e. that compassion alone is meaningless, a loathing of violence, especially when it is full of brutality and terrorizing – and this often results in a loathing for all forms of politics, a longing for freedom, a belief in the 'little man' or, conversely, a secretly aristocratic outlook.

This type of humanistic atheism can absorb virtually anything which potentially could have a constructive meaning for the human race. But since in real life love and compassion, friendship and a loathing of violence can only exist in a concrete situation without which they cannot have any specifically positive or negative meaning, the only way abstract humanistic atheism can hold its own is by worshipping one specific value and making a compromise in ordinary everyday life according to utilitarian considerations.

Anti-theism stems from an awareness of the strength, power and autonomy of man; it is not as clear about where man lacks sovereignty. Abstract humanistic atheism leads to emotion, and to a general vague awareness of the weakness and wretchedness of man; but it is not really capable of discovering the real source of man's strength. Anti-clericalists make their type of atheism absolute by turning it into a specific political standpoint; abstract humanists make certain general aspects of their atheism absolute, but have no feeling for politics – in fact they have an absolute loathing for politics.

But man cannot realize himself fully outside the political sphere.

7

The Marxist atheist: his atheism is not automatically anti-clerical or anti-theist. Admittedly, he is always a strong critic of political clericalism, and always will be so long as it upholds or defends the particular capitalist class interests of the bourgeoisie or identifies itself with these interests. He criticizes and always will criticize ecclesiastical policy whenever the Church makes no comment on criminal political actions, or dissociates itself from them in a far too general way, or too cautiously. He will always be highly critical whenever he comes up against anti-Communist feelings within the Churches. In a socialist country, a Marxist atheist will always be critical of the Christian Churches when they fail in their loyalty to the socialist state, to its constitution and its laws. He will also be critical when he observes that their whole attitude to life, their conception of politics and religion are moving away from the general human ideals and values which belong to true Christianity. The Marxist atheist will always step forward to criticize Christianity and the Christian Churches wherever they are not being sufficiently self-critical over questions concerning philosophy, history, social relationships and politics.

The Marxist atheist's critical attitude to the Christian Churches does not stem from a particular emotional antipathy or the need to persecute people 'of a different faith'. Criticism of its policies loses its point and its social justification as soon as Christianity comes to its senses and abandons all its political links with particular classes or reactionary ideas and social schemes; as soon as its theist motivation encourages it to make an effort to solve the current problems threatening mankind; and if it – even if it does this in its own way – makes an effort to eliminate the barriers which still separate man from his total dimension and frustrate all attempts to build up a social order in which man could develop himself as a 'commonwealth'.

The Marxist atheist will not, it is true, be able to accept the Christian's starting-point as the right one, nor will he be able to accept his goal; but with this proviso, he will take him seriously as a man, have confidence in him, will be able to discuss many things with him, examine various questions with him, argue with him, and fall silent. In so doing he is not abandoning his ideological criticism of the Churches, but will proceed instead, in association with the Christian, to perform those actions by which the believer wishes to serve the good of mankind or society on *his own* responsibility. Equally, the Marxist will expect him to back up his, the Marxist's, initiatives, actions, endeavours and efforts. In a socialist country, a Marxist atheist will initiate a friendly dialogue with the Christian in which he will request that he should endeavour to gain a real understanding of Communist policy, even if he knows that he will never become a Marxist or an atheist. He will not be concerned with trying to make him adapt himself out of opportunism. He is convinced that the more radical the manner in which the Christian pleads his cause the closer he will be able to get to socialism. This means that the Marxist's criticism of Christianity and the Christian Churches is a special type of class-conscious criticism; he objects to religions in so far as they are trying to pass off the interests of one particular class as generally binding, universal interests. He has no intention of defending the interests of the working class exclusively: for the special interests of the working class were and still are that they should be able to lay claim to the honorary title of mankind, and thus heal the breach which has opened up between the classes during the course of history. As long as this alone is the particular concern of the working class, and it comes up against particular and selfish class struggles, i.e. as long as the struggle to gain the universal honorary title of mankind is played out on the thorny ground of politics, Marxist atheism will continue to be a class-conscious and politically committed ideology. This is not to say that its current ideas about socialism and Communism have the validity of unchangeable dogmas. The actual way of working of the Communist Parties automatically disproves such an idea. But they are schemes which – though they are incomplete from the historical point of view – are characterized by that universal and also universally acceptable theory for which mankind is indebted to Marx. Developing these schemes in accordance with Marx's basic theory and making them concrete – that is what Communist policy is all about.

This means that anti-theism is not an essential component of Marxist atheism. A Marxist does not always and in all circumstances see religion as the 'opium of the people'. When he agrees with Marx in admitting that religion is on the one hand the expression of genuine suffering and on the other a protest against genuine suffering, he is also aware that this coupling of the religious with the social is conditioned by history. He knows – as does any Christian who is capable of taking a critical look at himself – that within the Christian religion there is a very marked tendency to convert everything into soothing words of consolation, in other words to find illusory solutions to problems. He is aware that if religion is anchored in the 'paradise of the heart' and the 'centre of certainty',[2] this does not only have an enervating effect when people want to draw on it for courage in conducting their everyday life. The Marxist atheist knows that in the last analysis even a protest motivated by religion can become a drug if it leads to a Christian-Socialist Utopia. But the Christian must not think of God as a prism in which the world is reflected, for God can also represent a direct call for a socially and humanly responsible decision to act. In that case, the concept of God loses its dreamlike quality and challenges men to action in human terms.

On the other hand, Marxism is not abstract humanistic atheism either, even though it is capable of understanding the universally human views of that type of atheism. The Marxist appreciates the efforts it makes, but he cannot sanction its way of looking at things, since this does not make allowances for class differences, and always leads its adherents back to Utopianism. Man is not merely an individual; we cannot think about him as a man except in abstract terms. Man as an individual comprises a totality of social relationships. Outside these relationships he ceases to be intelligible and important. He becomes a pure subjective identity, a consciousness, which does certainly know what it might or should be capable of, but does not know how it is to bring this about. Marx's historical materialism, on the other hand, starts from the fact that universal human emancipation is not to be arrived at via an act of consciousness, nor on the level of relationships between men which are understood in abstract terms – such as love, goodness, justice, etc.; but merely via practical action, which has an effect on history, and which separates the metabolism between men and nature in such a way that its efficiency and functionalism permanently ensure the universal evolution of man as a universal being. This action must accordingly make itself felt over long periods of history; and it must struggle during these periods, resolutely and often with much bloodshed, with those forces, classes, groups and nations which hold doggedly on to their own particular interests; it must also know that it is not easy and never will be easy to organize the administration of public affairs in such a way that every single person is guaranteed a measure of freedom which is constantly increasing.

Marx's historical materialism can lead us away from thinking in illusory terms, from attempting to fill men with false hopes, with consoling drugs which buoy them up with beautiful dreams. It is in other words atheistic; fundamentally atheistic.

It would be a mistake to conclude from this statement that Marxism is a form of 'theo-tropism'. Not at all: the Marxist atheist's preoccupation with God is merely his most distinctive trait, in the sense that he criticizes a religion which has not yet found itself or its authentic form. But for the Marxist, atheism is of its very nature the sole dimension of his thinking, of all his questions and answers. In this sense, one could see this type of atheism as the *first philosophy* in the Aristotelian sense, as Marxist metaphysics.

Footnotes

1) J. Krejči: 'Criteria for atheist education within the framework of ideological education in general and the education of young people in particular.' This study was submitted by the author to the Central Committee of the Communist Party of Czechoslovakia in 1966, but exists only in typescript form, in Czech. Cf. Krejči: '*Ein neues Modell des wissenschaftlichen Atheismus*', in *Internationale Dialog Zeitschrift 1: 1968*, part 2, pp. 191–207.

2) This is an allusion to one of the most important books by the Czech theologian and educationalist Jan Amos Komenský (Comenius) (1592–1670), *The Labyrinth of the World and the Paradise of the Heart* (*Layrint sveta a lustranz srdce*) (1631). An English translation by Count Lützow was published in London in 1901, new edition 1950.

4

MARXIST ATHEISM
AS METAPHYSICS

1

If Marx's atheism is ever to become what it was originally, it is essential that we should trace the narrowing down process which has relegated it to the level of a fringe line of reasoning.

And yet, to be a Marxist atheist involves nothing less than being an active member of that community which has drawn from the historical position held by the working class certain conclusions concerning the tangible prospects which await man, and mankind in general. This type of community must logically look at all problems in a radical and humane light, reject all forms of intervention from illusionary or religious thinking, and apply the same radical methods in solving the problems. If we consider the full extent of a free decision of this type, we will eventually come up with an attempt to formulate something which has always, by its very nature, been known in philosophy as metaphysics.

It must be stated from the very outset that any attempts to evolve a Marxist system of metaphysics cannot transform Marxism into some sort of new religion. Instead, it will become a form of metaphysics by transcending, or attempting to transcend, every type of illusion, including religious illusions.

But there is yet another doubt which must be dispelled. As far as a Marxist with an average level of education is concerned, metaphysics are the exact opposite of dialectics. If Marxists reflect on metaphysical questions, they will at best see this as inconsistent. Yet in so far as, say, Engels talks about metaphysics, what he has in mind is the type of reasoning which, in the wake of the objectively orientated science of the classical era, has gained ground as what is known as the 'common-sense' outlook, which says that things either exist or don't exist. In all those areas where reality slips away from this type of over-simplified comparison, 'sound common sense' is thrown into confusion and reaches beyond its own limits to find some sort of explanation, reaching its way towards some sort of presumed, supernatural powers. Thus Engels merely excludes bad metaphysics. He contrasts metaphysics with dialectics, seeing the latter as a negative process, which forces practical usage to transcend each *historical* stage at the moment when man's tendency to transform it into something *natural* increases. He thus outlines for our philosophical consideration the realm of genuine metaphysical problems, and at the same time points out the ways by which we can solve them without taking any risks.

Indeed it would be surprising if it were otherwise. Marxism is a practical philosophy, and as such it opens up new ground for thought and practical human activity at every historical phase reached by the militant working class, and in the broadest sense by mankind in general. It is always forcing us at the turning-points to reformulate the basic questions all over again, and to search for new and more appropriate answers. The problems which are generally known as the 'eternal' problems of mankind are not eternal because they are permanently being dragged around by the whole of mankind, or because men always produce *ad nauseam* the same old answers. Quite the reverse: they are eternal because they are continually being posed in a new way, and because new possibilities of solving them are always cropping up.

In this sense, metaphysics represents in objective terms a social requirement. Mankind evolves by transcending itself, and by transforming the limits set for it by nature into historical limits, thanks to man's many-sided practical activity. This means that metaphysics represents the reflective aspect, or alternatively the theoretical aspect, of practical behaviour. This statement may well give an indication of the subject-matter with which metaphysics is concerned. It deliberates on the problem of the type of subjective identity which transcends itself, and yet at the same time is constantly threatened with being changed back into something dead, with being swallowed up once again by insatiable nature, and thus losing its meaning for mankind. Yet at the same time it is also menaced by another danger: that of being so afraid of ending up like this that it will withdraw into its own exclusiveness and gamble away all its opportunities by its own speculative enterprises.

Atheism as Marxist metaphysics represents an attempt to formulate a theory of subjective identity which would not be subjectivist, a theory of transcendence, of overstepping-one's-own-limits, which would not be objective.

This form of metaphysics is embodied in every facet of Marxism, though it is never explicitly expressed. But the main idea underlying it is outlined in several places: e.g. in the essays on Ludwig Feuerbach, in the *Economic and Philosophical Manuscripts* dating from 1844, in the *Communist Manifesto*, in the summary and whole first draft of *Das Kapital*, and elsewhere.

The historical circumstances and the concrete requirements of the class struggle have emerged despite the fact that this aspect of Marxism has never before been thrown into relief as forcibly as it has today. This means that we are clearly once again embarking on a truly momentous philosophical effort, which is of decisive importance for the development of Marxism, for the growth of its appeal and for building up its long-term plans for society. The following reflections cannot lay any claims to the glorious title of Marxist metaphysics; nor are they intended as such. They are an as yet highly unsystematic attempt at reflecting on specific topics, and thrashing them out as openly and frankly as possible. The author senses, and is in his heart of hearts fully aware, that they underlie all that has already been said in the form of a series of unspoken questions.

2

Through the infinite cosmos, which is governed by laws which must be obeyed, rolls the dark terrestrial globe – through infinite space, through infinite time, a vast dark, frosty infinity – and on this globe there skips about a little band of creatures with hypertrophically developed brains, kicking up a racket in its highly infinite time with repeated cries of: 'We have conquered the earth, we will tame the seas, we will govern nature, we will subdue the universe!' – and the earth rolls on through infinite space, following its inevitable laws and taking no notice of the squeaks coming from the mice – or from mankind.

This passage appeared in one of our newspapers recently. It is a depressing picture, and one glance at it undoes all our inspirations and our whole history, including that which is yet to come. As a final and definitive answer it is unacceptable, as far as mankind is concerned. But we must concede its validity as a question. After all it crops up in a less spectacular form whenever – as happens often enough – Marxists are asked what is going to come after Communism.

We put forward a whole series of reasons why such a question cannot be asked, and yet it keeps on cropping up over and over again. So let us try to see what exactly the concrete problem underlying this question is.

The questioner will not be satisfied if we merely paint a picture of the future in the most rosy terms. What interests him is what sort of future *that* future has. He would like to know about the motives which are supposed to inspire him to feel committed to the future; i.e. he knows that it is highly probable that he will no longer be alive to see it, but even if he did live to see it, would he not find himself faced with a new future, which would compel him to ask all over again: what next?

This is a succinct and radical way of asking why each one of us should be in favour of Communism. Why should we sacrifice our lives, the few years at our disposal, to this idea, to this human perspective, to this social schema? Perhaps it is so that our children and our children's children can live better than ourselves? So that they will no longer be threatened by atom bombs, famine or any other catastrophe? What guarantee is there that such a result is possible? And even if we did achieve it, would our offspring really live better? What assurances have we that they will not come off badly in their one and only life? But if no such assurances exist, is there any point in advocating this goal? Why should men expend their energies on some far distant future instead of enjoying life as it is today? Why should they keep on postponing the realization of the dreams in which they long for a better future, thinking of life in the present as something inferior, which can easily be sacrificed, indeed must perhaps be sacrificed? Why should we think of something which has yet to happen as more real and more important than what is already here, when it is not even certain that it will ever happen? Isn't this just a form of Utopianism? Aren't we simply replacing one belief with another?

To the Marxist, all this represents a challenge. There is no situation in which he *could* avoid accepting it. There is no reason why he *should* avoid it.

3

The future: is it true that the Marxist or the Communist sees it in such absolute terms that he thinks of the present as already sacrificed to the future? Is it true that he conceives of the present as a purely material basis, with no intrinsic value? There was never a clear-cut answer to this question in the days of revolutionary Marxism. There were harsh periods in history which demanded sacrifices for the sake of socialism, or for the maintenance of a mode of existence worthy of the human race; periods which swallowed up whole generations. We should not be surprised if, in the eyes of those who have made the sacrifice, Communism has taken on the form of an absolute goal, compared to which everything else, even they themselves, has become a mere means to an end. Setting oneself a concrete goal was on a par with making the concrete sacrifices demanded in the history of the class struggle. This type of historical situation can by its very nature crop up over and over again.

This makes it all the more necessary that we should as far as possible avoid creating illusions. Neither socialism nor Communism can be seen as an absolute goal in the sense that compared with them everything else becomes a mere means to an end; nor in the sense that they will be a final state for mankind, since that is the only case where this type of instrumental view of the present would be justified. Nor, finally, in the sense that the future of Communism might already be an *absolute* historical certainty, so that our present active existence would not matter too much. The point is rather that the value of the present, as an end in itself, lies in what we make of it, and it is only thus that it can become a suitable or unsuitable means of attaining this goal.

But what we make of our present is identical with what we make

of ourselves, within the structure of the community to which we
belong in concrete terms. The thought of the future, of socialism,
represents for the Marxist the structural principle underlying this
conscious creative act. It is a strange principle: it proclaims that it
is not absolutely, and therefore never totally, enforceable, and is
also historically not completely secure.

This means in practical terms that the Marxist atheist is not confronted with an absolute future, but with an open future: open in
the sense of offering every possible opportunity to man, but also in
the sense that it remains uncertain whether it can ever come to
anything, indeed whether it will ever happen. Any glimpse of the
future always has an element of uncertainty; and uncertainty is one
of the essential questions underlying the very existence of modern
man: it is not certain whether the future will outlive its current
historical stage as an appallingly makeshift arrangement; this
means that the prospects for Communism are not absolutely certain either. We believe in it and work for it, but certainty pure and
simple really doesn't come into it.

Should we be writing about it?

Should we be keeping quiet about it?

It is not a question of our reflections on the subject leading us
into this state of uncertainty. The point is rather that we ponder on
it because it is *staring us in the face*.

The world of today is indeed a makeshift sort of place. After all
we find this out every time we examine the process by which the
scientific-cum-technical revolution got under way, and also every
time we define our own age as the age of the transition from
capitalism to Communism, as an intermediate stage between two
historical eras. Two different processes interpenetrate each other
here, each making the other more complicated. The shapes and
structures of social life and the life of the individual are no more
than provisional structures. This provisional quality tells us a thing
or two about the most important prospects, but it also tells us,
given the class situation in today's society, about the existential
uncertainty which underlies our world. People have a feeling that
the earth is constantly quaking beneath their feet. They do admittedly foresee that seismic shocks will occur at some point, but

they don't know when, and so they sleep outside in the open air, outside the doubtful safety of their own walls. They are well on the way to surrendering to the dangers of catastrophes and annihilation.

Where are we supposed to gather the strength, the urge and the courage to act, when it looks as if every step forward merely increases the overall instability? And how are we to prevent the spread of a destructive scepticism, of that appalling apathy which runs 'I only live once, so I intend to live now'?

Moralizing appeals are not much good in the face of that sort of attitude. It is obvious that objective changes in reality do no immediate good either. Surmounting this provisional state is a lengthy process. But there is, all the same, a movement, an avant garde which is aware of the provisional nature of our world from the outset, and is continuously struggling against it.

The innermost motives underlying the behaviour of such people are not inspired by any sort of Messianic thinking, nor by a Utopian belief that Communism is mankind's port of call among the islands of paradise. They arise instead from the effort to find out what the man who has a right to the honorary title of 'man' is like.

4

Marxism, precisely because it is also atheism, knows that man possesses no more than two basic pieces of insight into himself of which he is absolutely certain: I am a social being who is capable of transcending himself; I know with absolute certainty that I must die.

These two certainties presuppose each other: because I am mortal, I am a social entity; society can live, evolve and become more humane, while its individual members die off. That is a form of dependence which is exclusively human.

But at the same time these two certainties are highly contradictory: death robs me of everything, even myself, but society will survive. Since it is permanently saddled with the death of its members, the life of society is never absolutely secure, and thence never absolutely complete either.

My death represents for me personally the end of all my hopes, but at the same time it represents hope for others, for society. And by the same token: life in society consists, precisely for this reason, of the permanent surmounting of disillusionment and hopelessness.

There are two ways of getting round this contradiction: we can either ascribe an absolute value to the life of the individual; or alternatively, we can allow it to be entirely absorbed into the human collectivity which is destined to outlive it. The individual is replaceable. Anyone who thinks himself irreplaceable is under a misapprehension. If, on the other hand, society declares that the individual is replaceable, objections are raised. Compared to society, the individual must always rank as irreplaceable. The *irreplaceability* of the individual is virtually the precondition of society, and may not be done away with.

The theories concerning subjective identity, whose adherents did not wish to take this in, lapsed into subjectivism: they reflected on the individual outside his connections with society, and arrived at the premise that there must be an immortal soul, an eternity and a God. If they wanted to avoid this fiction, they would enthuse instead about the eternal nature of society. In the first case, man could not transcend himself until his own death: through death he would realize himself for all eternity. All that was pious self-deception. In the second case, death was declared to be null and void, and in this way the realization of social schemes took on an appearance of finality and permanence – and thus was transformed by its very nature into something null and void, and a destructive form of disappointment set in.

The Marxist theory of subjective identity and transcendence is materialistic and dialectic.

Both the individual and mankind in general as they entered history are subjective. The individual, the 'ego', refuses to be reduced to a mere sum of social relationships, because it is also a focal point in which these relationships come together and alter; society in its turn is a subjective identity, not merely as the sum of its individuals, but as an everlasting fire in which new flames are constantly blazing up to replace the old ones which have burnt themselves out.

This image should not be taken as the expression of a cheap form of optimism. Individual death means *my* death, there is no getting round that. It represents my certainty for the future, and is basically the only totally certain event in man's life. But its burden, its tragedy, everything which caused human life to be called 'grief about eternity', does not only result from the purely individual, but from the fact that we are *involved* in supra-individual relationships. An animal, even a baby at the breast who cannot yet speak, does not experience this grief in the face of death. It is restricted to people involved in the community. So we will never get anywhere with our reflections on death (except in mysticism) unless we consider at the same time the individual's links with society.

I die – i.e. I will not complete my work, I will no longer see those I have loved, I will no longer experience beauty or sorrow. The unrepeatable music of this world will no longer find an echo in my senses; I will never again transcend myself, in any direction. All that I have left is this one last step.

The horror of *death* comes from *this* loss of connections: our innermost heart ceases to be the point of intersection where things come together. It becomes all the more inevitable that I should have this certainty in my individual future consciously present before me; that I should live in such a way that I put the maximum amount of my life into every relationship in which I am involved: as though I were going to die tomorrow.

Anyone who believes in God and the immortality of the soul always has hope, even in his last short hour of life; he will postpone his death just for a few more minutes. I do not have this hope. So I see all my relationships with transparent clarity, not obscured by mystic and illusory anticipation of something which will follow that ultimate fading away. Each of my relationships bears the mark of death. Each has a unique value in my eyes, and cannot be exchanged for another. Every encounter with one of my fellow-men is to me, who am myself a finite individual, a gift, for it may be my last encounter with him. And I too am a gift for anyone, provided that I have something to offer.

With regard to the individual, the atheistic theory of subjective identity bears the imprint of the fact of death and of meditation on this fact; yet it is not a theory of destructive hopelessness.

Rather the reverse. It is the place where the subjective identity first sees the light of day, in the form of an activity which reaches beyond itself, is hopeful because it affords hope, is sought out because it is itself searching, and is given gifts because it itself gives gifts. Only the individual who is aware of the certainty of his death *in this way* can become socially non-interchangeable. I myself have no hope of eternity and am at the mercy of death, but I represent hope for others who will outlive me: when my life comes to an end, the sum of what remains is the indispensable precondition of their life. It is true that their lives will also end in the same hopelessness. But it is only at this high price, at the price of personal defeat, that hope can be kept alive as one of the unalterable factors of human existence in general, as society's hope for the future.

We are all confronted by defeat the very moment we are born; in spite of this, hope continues among men; this is a paradox, but it is also evidence of man's social nature. Everything in us urges us not to acknowledge death, i.e. everything with which we as individual subjective identities are not yet socially integrated. This is obviously where theistic views originate.

But it is only when we take upon us this human destiny that we become men in the real sense of the word: creatures who are capable of upholding through thick and thin the hope of mankind, and indeed mankind itself, with all its plans, schemes and battles, and in the last analysis with all its illusions and fabrications.

This means that the following statement is valid: If we take death upon us as the future of which each individual is certain, every choice and decision that we make is given a new and radical orientation, i.e. that of going beyond ourselves to our fellows, to the community.

The worst part about death is not that it robs us of the inanimate objects we have acquired and places them in other hands. We ought at any rate to realize throughout our lives that that is not the worst part. The thing which is hard to bear is that it also robs us of what we have become, of our own individual self-realization. This means that we *can* understand if someone wants to retain his identity even after death. But we cannot ourselves adopt this outlook, unless we ultimately renounce the honorary title of 'man', and thus voluntarily rob ourselves of the possibility of transcending any barriers whatever in our lifetime. Yet the greater the objective human value of those things of which death robs us (for it also robs us of our illusions about our own value), the greater ultimately our personal defeat, and the greater also the significance of whatever remains embodied in the surviving supra-individual structures. The sum of men's hopes increases by this same amount.

But it would be wrong to take comfort from this correlation, seeing it as a means of reconciling the individual with the inevitable.

In point of fact there is something far worse than this defeat.

5

Practical activity lies at the centre of Marxist philosophy. It is the negation of both of the long-standing philosophical theories – the cosmic theory of antiquity and the historical theory of the Jews – and at the same time raises both of them to a higher level. The practical, active subjective identity divides up the cosmos by stepping out of its own narrow framework, discovering new continents, climbing up to the heights, and digging down to the depths. It hoists its flags on the mountain-tops and deposits its emblems on the celestial bodies. The scope of its power expands from day to day, and it feels that everything is attainable. It is merely a question of the means of doing so. It surveys the space it has conquered and experiences the delightful sensation of victory: power, greatness, glory. But at the same time, while continuing to stride through space, it is always coming up against some new barrier. It not only has constantly to overcome the resistance of the object world, but must also overcome its own time.

That is why any reality that we have acquired fades rapidly away within us. In the very moment of victory we suffer defeat. We see the whole time how powerless we are, how small and pitiful.

We gradually find out that all we have done is to defer something which can never be done away with altogether. Realization is more than mere success, the complete realization of our self, the highest expression of our being, a moment when uneasiness dies away and the last doubts leave us.

Every realization is also a disappointment: it reminds us that there is a limit, time, death.

In the very moment of victory we are exposed to an even more terrible threat – that we might die earlier than we really do die, before death has become a natural necessity. The real horror lies in just such a *premature* death, a death after which we go on living for many years.

The point is that as soon as we no longer want to modify the victory we have won in terms of time, we declare that it is a final victory over death. But we have thus become superfluous as far as society is concerned, because we no longer possess even the merest shadow of hope for others. We are, of course, still alive: we go on earning money, going to the theatre, taking part in sport, enjoying ourselves, loving, going to the seaside, being involved in politics; but we are without hope. We stop being ourselves. We become slaves to heteronomy: to the alien law of 'circumstances', of triviality, of worries which drag on and on, of our own Utopias, and of God. Without noticing it, we are gradually decaying. So we endeavour to see to it that our work is not wrested away from us until the very last moment, that we do not suffer defeat until the very end, when there really is no way of avoiding the issue. This will cause us such a lot of trouble, and require such tenacity in the face of death as it begins to affect us, that, as long as we don't give up, we can 'become somebody' in the eyes of our fellow-men. We will work as though we were destined to be here for ever. And then when death really does come, we are more than ever before. We 'are' more.

So the defeat is all the greater. The tragedy of it cannot be spirited away; but it is the source of man's hope.

Life – death.

6

So life and death are not merely physical realities, but are spatial-cum-temporal relationships, with references to the subjective identity of a specially human nature, in which the individual is in practice constantly stepping over to join the totality of humanity, as it stands before us in its appropriate historical form, and vice versa.

It only remains to consider what motive enables us to take death upon us in this conscious, reflective way, and yet in so doing remain human: a motive which does not need either the pain-killing solace of spiritualism, or the forgetfulness of self which hides behind objects, but remains materialistic and atheistic.

We might possibly ask at this point what sort of historical strength the great liberal movements have built up. We are used to looking beneath subjective motives to find the objective driving-forces underlying them; these are what motivates the masses, rather than individuals, and in fact they do not do so in random situations, but at the decisive turning-points in history. So we must initially proceed methodologically. Otherwise we can scarcely do more than get a grip on isolated qualities of the epoch-making activity of man. But this does not exclude the other question: what prism has the subjective identity, which is to be understood in historical terms, used to absorb deep within itself these objective driving-forces? What is the driving force which moves man inwardly to take the tragedy of his own defeat consciously upon himself, for the sake of a communal hope for mankind?

The following type of answer clearly will not satisfy us: the common good, better days ahead, the idea of sacrifice and growing awareness, an ideal, the dream of the future, justice, freedom – for all these are already, or so it seems at any rate, second-class motives into which the subjective identity integrates itself.

What were the deep-seated inner motives which inspired a man to enter the Communist Party in difficult times? A loathing of the inhumane situation around him? A vision of a world without class conflict? A feeling of solidarity with the oppressed and the exploited?

Undoubtedly. And then there is also a rational awareness of the way in which men could shake off their former history. The study of the inherent laws underlying the course of history, expert scientific deliberation which discovers ways and means which are supposed to be appropriate to man and to the objective issues; in short — knowledge.

And yet we have a feeling that there is something more basic than this.

We mean the human, and inter-human relationship which has always traditionally borne the name of 'love'.

We are afraid of the word. It is too ceremonious. Too often abused.

And yet we still take it into consideration, though we do not think in terms of the transformation of Christianity into a religious myth, a transformation which stemmed from the time of Jesus; nor are we thinking of the deification of love which came from Feuerbach and many others after him. We are equally far removed from their sentimental interpretation and from their unsentimental one.

We do not mean by this the 'moral law within us', or the Utopian-type branch of ethics which says that everyone is to love each other.

In this type of reflection we interpret it as the imperative Existential precondition of all human relationships: as the key to its make-up, a key which is in the hands of the subjective identity wherever it wishes to let concrete relationships and its own inner life ring harmoniously together; as the code word which allows work to become creative and creativeness to become man's self-realization, both in the case of individuals, and for whole historical movements. This definition does not preclude the existence of conflict, of class war; it steers clear of any kind of pacifism, whether directed against war or against ideological conflict. Let me repeat: I understand love as one element in the make-up of the subjective identity, whenever it decides to perform an act of immediate interest and endeavours to give this decision the optimum human form. This can consist equally well of pronouncing the death sentence over somebody else, or of sacrificing one's own life; everything which lies between these two extremes will do, but it can never contain any element which would take away man's right to the honorary title of 'man'.

If looked at in this way, love is truly boundless, as far as its human potentialities are concerned: but this should not be understood in abstract terms, as though it were valid 'at all times, regardless of place, time, rank, age or sex', etc.; it should not be understood as an easily roused emotion, which flares up only to die down again soon after.

Love is limitless in that it possesses in practical terms an enormous number of possibilities; in that whenever it *really* is, whenever it is realized in a decision and later in an action, it possesses its own unique, non-interchangeable and non-repeatable value; and also in that we can never say: we will never again embark on anything new, never again compose a new melody; everything has already happened, and everything which is happening now is only a repetition, a non-transferable and spectacular one perhaps, but definitely no more than a repetition.

When understood in this way, love is *bottomless*: it is unfathomable in that the man who resolves to perform an action for the good of society can never say that he got to the bottom of it, unless he has allowed this key to be snatched away from him prematurely before his real end.

Love is an 'eternal' theme because it is the principle underlying creation, man's practical activity in history *par excellence*.

As such it represents the transition from 'I' to 'we' and vice versa. It is only in this transcendence that love between 'I' and 'thou', love as expressed in romantic literature, acquires its real value, rids itself of the individualistic limitation which eventually destroys it as love. The 'thou' whom we love opens the door to human relationships, because he or she clearly leads us to our maximum potential.

As creative activity in itself, love is an adventurous business: by summoning up our courage to take part in this concrete creative process, we also summon up enough courage to accept a love which will only be possible in the future. Genuine love always transcends our present potential. Which is why it is so difficult; it contains drama, tension, despair, hope, faith – all those elements which go hand in hand with the radical decision to step across the river of time.

Love is wonderful in the literal sense of the word: it suspends the causality of nature by giving it a human stamp. It also suspends it in the species of animate beings whom we call 'men' – it gives them the gift of culture.

Love is difficult: it is always closely bound up with death. But it is easy and a matter of course if we have consciously taken the burden upon us.

In the end we will suffer defeat, but we will not rob our survivors of any of that element which makes the life of the human community a perpetual drama, a struggle, a conflict, not excepting the ultimate defeat.

We will not lessen their hope for a community offering a life worthy of man. We call this hope Communism.

That is why we do not believe in God, although it is absurd.

INDEX

Abelard, Peter, 71
Acts of the Apostles, 36–7
Adam (and Eve), 29, 31
Aeterni Patris (encyclical), 121
Alexander the Great, 60, 61
Anglicans, 105
annihilation, 8
'anonymous Christian', 140–42, 144
anthropology in relation to theology, 168–73
anti-clericalism, 174, 175, 193–5
anti-theism, 195, 197
Apocalypse, 37, 43–6, 50, 60
Apocrypha, 23
Aquinas, St Thomas, *see* St Thomas Aquinas
Aquino, Landulf, 65
Aristotelian philosophy, 26, 59, 61, 92, 93, 94, 96; effect on St Thomas Aquinas, 74–5
atheism, 10, 88, 113; abstract humanist atheist, 195–7; anti-clericalism, 174, 175, 193–5; anti-theism, 195, 197; attitude to the Bible, 22; attitude of the modern theologian Pierre Teilhard de Chardin, 140; conformist atheist, 191–3; historical considerations, 154; history of, 158–67; influences in spreading of, 183–7; Marxist, 157, 198–201; Marxist, as metaphysics, 203–18; Marxist view of death, 209–14, 215;

Marxist view of the future, 207–9; practical atheists, 187–91; reasons for existence, 180–200; scientifically motivated, 153–7; sociological surveys, 181–3; sources, 150–54; types of atheist, 187–200; within socialism, 149–57
Augustinius, Aurelius, 53

Babel, Isaac, 143
baptism, 110
Barbarossa, Frederick, 65
Bauer, Bruno, 103
Bible, examination of, 21–33; examination by Marxism, 16–17; Old Testament, 23–33
bourgeois rationalism, 122–5

Calvinists, 105
Carthage, St Augustine's life in, 54, 55
'Catholic', 68
Catholic *see* Roman Catholic Church
Chardin, Pierre Teilhard de, 135
charity, Jesus's doctrine of, 48–9; *see also* love
Chenu, Marie-Dominique, 131, 132
Children of Israel, 32, 40
choice, idea of, 32, 33
Christian democracy, 126–7, 186
Christianity, 14–15, 34, 143–5, 162–4; adaptation to contemporary circumstances,

219

Index

Index